Peer Participation and Software

D0095947

This report was made possible by the grants from the John D. and Catherine T. MacArthur Foundation in connection with its grant-making initiative on Digital Media and Learning. For more information on the initiative visit www.macfound.org.

The John D. and Catherine T. MacArthur Foundation Reports on Digital Media and Learning

Peer Participation and Software: What Mozilla Has to Teach Government by David R. Booth

The Future of Learning Institutions in a Digital Age by Cathy N. Davidson and David Theo Goldberg with the assistance of Zoë Marie Jones

The Future of Thinking: Learning Institutions in a Digital Age by Cathy N. Davidson and David Theo Goldberg with the assistance of Zoë Marie Jones

New Digital Media and Learning as an Emerging Area and "Worked Examples" as One Way Forward by James Paul Gee

Living and Learning with New Media: Summary of Findings from the Digital Youth Project by Mizuko Ito, Heather Horst, Matteo Bittanti, danah boyd, Becky Herr-Stephenson, Patricia G. Lange, C. J. Pascoe, and Laura Robinson with Sonja Baumer, Rachel Cody, Dilan Mahendran, Katynka Z. Martínez, Dan Perkel, Christo Sims, and Lisa Tripp

Young People, Ethics, and the New Digital Media: A Synthesis from the GoodPlay Project by Carrie James with Katie Davis, Andrea Flores, John M. Francis, Lindsay Pettingill, Margaret Rundle, and Howard Gardner

Confronting the Challenges of Participatory Culture: Media Education for the 21st Century by Henry Jenkins (P.I.) with Ravi Purushotma, Margaret Weigel, Katie Clinton, and Alice J. Robison

The Civic Potential of Video Games by Joseph Kahne, Ellen Middaugh, and Chris Evans

Peer Production and Software

What Mozilla Has to Teach Government

David R. Booth

The MIT Press
Cambridge, Massachusetts
London, England

For information about special quantity discounts, please email special_sales@mitpress.mit.edu.

This book was set in Stone Sans and Stone Serif by the MIT Press. Printed and bound in the United States of America.

Library of Congress Cataloging-in-Publication Data

Booth, David, 1945–
Peer participation and software : what Mozilla has to teach government / David R. Booth.
    p. cm.—(The John D. and Catherine T. MacArthur Foundation Reports on Digital Media and Learning)
Includes bibliographical references.
ISBN 978-0-262-51461-3 (pbk. : alk. paper)
1. Computer software—Development—Social aspects. 2. Digital media—Social aspects. 3. Netscape Mozilla. I. Title.
QA76.76.D47B67   2010   302.23'1—dc22   2009042932

10   9   8   7   6   5   4   3   2   1

Contents

Series Foreword

The John D. and Catherine T. MacArthur Foundation Reports on Digital Media and Learning, published by the MIT Press, in collaboration with the Monterey Institute for Technology and Education (MITE), present findings from current research on how young people learn, play, socialize, and participate in civic life. The Reports result from research projects funded by the MacArthur Foundation as part of its $50 million initiative in digital media and learning. They are published openly online (as well as in print) in order to support broad dissemination and to stimulate further research in the field.

Introduction

Firefox is a free Web browser developed by the Mozilla Foundation for Windows, Linux, and Mac and in use by an estimated 270 million people worldwide.[1] As of December 2008, Firefox had garnered over 21 percent of browser market share, while Microsoft's Internet Explorer dropped below 70 percent of the market for the first time in eight years.[2] In maintaining and improving the Firefox browser, Mozilla depends not only on its core team of professional programmers and managers, but also on a network of volunteer technologists and enthusiasts—free/libre and open source software (FLOSS) developers—who contribute their expertise. Firefox is a unique example of peer production both for its vast scale and for its combination of structured, hierarchical management with open, collaborative volunteer participation.

The purpose of this report is to address how and why the Mozilla Foundation is successful at organizing large-scale participation in the development of its software. What motivates Mozilla to solicit the expertise of anyone who wishes to provide her time and knowledge to the Mozilla enterprise? What motivates volunteers to participate?

In examining the answers to these questions, the goal is to explore what aspects of Mozilla's open source approach to software development are transferable to government and civil society. Broadly speaking, the term *open source software* refers to software placed in the public domain by its proprietors as an invitation for outside programmers to volunteer their expertise to improving that software. The correlations between open source software and participatory governance come into sharper focus when considering the fact that Mozilla extends the open source idea beyond programming: Firefox's user community helps with marketing campaigns, responds to queries on Mozilla message boards, and writes and edits documentation for developers.

Mozilla's commitment to collaborating with its browser users on marketing, public relations, and product education suggests parallels with the Obama administration's philosophy of participatory governance (which amplifies the much older Jeffersonian ideal of democratic participation). Mozilla's success at engendering part-time, volunteer participation that produces successful marketplace innovation suggests strategies for how to organize civic participation in communities and government. Specifically, the Mozilla approach might demonstrate how to galvanize participation by those in the technical community. More generally, Mozilla's open source model may have something to teach us about how to create successful participatory democracy.

This report is divided into five sections. The first, Open Source, introduces the Mozilla Foundation, beginning with its inception as Netscape Communications and culminating with its present open-source business model. This brief history helps to define open source by explaining Mozilla's place in the open source community.

The second section, Open Source at Mozilla, summarizes the unique mix of hierarchical management with peer-produced, volunteer labor that enables Mozilla to operate at scale in the development of the Firefox browser. To understand how volunteer contributions of code are evaluated and incorporated into ongoing projects, open source participants are identified on the basis of their roles in a system of distributed peer review.

The third section, Licensing, discusses the rules under which open source developers maintain and improve the Firefox browser. The role of licensing in open-source software development and distribution is examined with an eye toward the freedom and limitations granted the licensee: What protocols do volunteer developers follow in participating in projects at Mozilla? How does the Mozilla Foundation govern the redistribution of its source code? What role does licensing play in helping to bring about volunteer participation? How does an open source license actually legislate the freedom that makes large-scale participation possible? How does licensing create incentives to form communities?

In section four, Beyond Software, we explain how Mozilla takes the modular nature of code writing and applies these same techniques to a range of nontechnical activities. The utilization of an international community of volunteers in the strategic marketing of software is unique to the Mozilla Foundation and suggests the most parallels with civic engagement.

We begin the last and longest section of the report, What Software Has to Teach Government, with two questions: (1) Why is Mozilla successful? and (2) Is the Mozilla methodology repeatable? We apply the answers to these questions to several contemporary examples of participatory governance in the United States. We then examine the Obama administration's efforts to solicit public participation both during the election campaign and in the early days of the new presidency. In concluding this report with recommendations for further research on participatory governance, we address possible shortcomings in the Mozilla methodology as applied to the work of government.

Open Source

"Free" vs. "Open Source" Software

In 1995, three years before its acquisition by AOL, Netscape Communications marked its initial public offering with a plan to distribute its browser, Netscape Communicator (formerly Navigator), at no cost. Netscape would have gone forward with the free distribution of its software application if its financial backers (in the mid-1990s) hadn't stipulated that the product generate revenue. Netscape acquiesced, while at the same time distributing the browser free of charge to students, educators, and researchers. It would be three years before Netscape would give the browser away to everyone, "no strings attached."[3]

It was also in 1998, following the precedent set by Linus Torvalds when he developed Linux, a Unix-like operating system, with input from unaffiliated programmers from around the world, that Netscape published the source code for Netscape Communicator under an open source license. This meant that anyone with enough programming expertise and enthusiasm could modify and redistribute the source code.

Colloquially known as "hackers," members of MIT's Tech Model Railroad Club (TMRC) and the MIT Artificial Intelligence Laboratory had championed such rights since the 1960s. Richard Stallman further galvanized the hacker subculture in 1983 by creating the GNU Project—GNU stands for "GNU's Not Unix"—and founding the Free Software Movement (FSM). In announcing the GNU Project, Stallman declared the development of "a sufficient body of free software . . . to get along without any software that is not free."[4] While for Stallman "free" also means "free of charge," his adherents emphasize liberty over cost: as they are wont to say, "free as in speech, not as in beer." Today, the organization born out of the FSM, the Free Software Foundation (FSF), defines free software on the basis of the following tenets, as published in the GNU manifesto:[5]

- The freedom to run the program, for any purpose (freedom 0).
- The freedom to study how the program works, and adapt it to your needs (freedom 1). Access to the source code is a precondition for this.
- The freedom to redistribute copies so you can help your neighbor (freedom 2).
- The freedom to improve the program, and release your improvements (and modified versions in general) to the public, so that the whole community benefits (freedom 3). Access to the source code is a precondition for this.

The proliferation of manifestos by contemporary technologists—*The Hacker's Manifesto* (1986) by Lloyd Blankenship and *The Cathedral and the Bazaar* (1997) by Eric S. Raymond, to name two—echoes a history of credos in political life from the

United States Declaration of Independence to the Republican Party's 1994 Contract with America; and in the arts, including Walt Whitman's 1885 preface to *Leaves of Grass* and Frank O'Hara's *Personism: A Manifesto*, from the world of poetry, suggesting hackers deploy a self-conscious political and social activism. And certainly the FSF was (and is) activist. What it was not conceived as, though, was a business model. Instead, the FSF articulated a philosophy, one predicated on the ideal that software, *morally* speaking, should not be proprietary.

By 1992, having formulated and executed the GNU Project under the guiding principles of the FSF, Stallman combined his community-developed operating system components with the Linux *kernel*—code that manages communications between software and hardware in an operating system—to create an operating system comprised of entirely free software. Though this accomplishment was not the first of its kind, it aids our description of a seemingly natural transition from free software as primarily a manifesto to open source software, based on a similarly altruistic ideology, with real product and commercial potential. (Anticipating the software industry as we know it today, it's worth noting that in the early 1990s the availability of the Linux kernel gave rise to several Linux distributions when developers of Unix-like operating systems built on top of the Linux kernal. Early examples of Linux distributions include MCC Interim Linux and TAMU. Founded in mid-1992, Softlanding Linux System [SLS] was the first Linux distribution to include more than the kernel and basic utilities.[6] Announced in November 1992, Yggdrasil Linux/GNU/X purportedly was the first Linux distribution widely available to the public.[7] Linux distributions that are well known today include Fedora, Debian, Gentoo Linux, and Red Hat.)

In early 1997, in anticipation of Netscape's release of its source code, Bruce Perens and Eric S. Raymond founded the Open Source Initiative (OSI), an organization committed to the advocacy of software with freely available source code. The OSI definition of open software shares core values with the FSF definition of free software; namely, the software user enjoys the right to use, modify, and redistribute source code under the terms of one of a number of sanctioned licensing agreements.[8] Those agreements all grant users these core freedoms and license many of the rights that copyright owners legally possess. Famously, the General Public License (GPL) "infects" any modification to code licensed under it with the same open source requirements. Nevertheless, the founding of the OSI inaugurated a public debate about the ethical contrasts between "free" and "open" in software development.

Whereas the FSF maintained that open-source software development as an organizational strategy for increasing market share threatened to blur the distinctions between free and proprietary software, the OSI held that "it was time to dump the moralizing and confrontational attitude that had been associated with 'free software' in the past and sell the idea strictly on the same pragmatic, business-case grounds that had motivated Netscape."[9] When on March 31, 1998, Netscape released the source code for the Communicator suite, it did so to compete with Microsoft's Internet Explorer browser. Netscape's intention was to make up in advertising what it lost from the sale of software licenses.

Some Pros and Cons of Open Source

The benefits of open source software typically cited focus on business rationales. They include the argument that open source is often (but not always) less expensive than proprietary software. Another advantage of open source software is that it can be more customized by the end-user. As such, open source is arguably more educational than proprietary software, in that the user is invited to learn or practice coding or both. He does so for his own benefit and, when customizations are profound and implemented into new versions of widely distributed software, for the benefit of the community at large. (As we will soon discuss at length, Mozilla is somewhat atypical in that it uses the open source practice not only as a way of deepening its pool of talented programmers, but also as a mechanism for increasing public participation in the maintenance of the Internet as "a global public resource that must remain open and accessible."[10] Ideological in nature, this tenet is fundamental to our understanding of the Mozilla business model as relevant to participatory governance at large.)

Because open source software can be copied and shared without a fee and without violating intellectual property laws, users can operate software essential to their jobs at home, and teachers can send their students home with the software in use in the classroom. Because the licensee in open source development is free to modify and redistribute software, license management is simplified. Licensors dedicate fewer resources to the problem of piracy. As a safeguard against commercial exploitation of the source code, the GPL obliges those who modify the code to share their improvements with the community. The specifics of open source licensing will be explored in a later section of this report.

Open source software also creates networks between an organization's in-house developers and unaffiliated developers. Apache, a program that hosts nearly half of the Web sites on the Internet, facilitates a network comprising itself, Web designers, and Web site proprietors. A company like Apple can build its latest operating system on the source code of BSD, an open source operating system, as a way of keeping pace with community-based innovations in this product category. If a software company goes out of business, the community still has the source code and can interface with other vendors and developers. Even if a vendor remains solvent, the community may avoid being locked into doing business with that vendor.

There are counterfactuals to these assertions. Open source is not always cheaper. The opportunity costs of open source software can be significant if a program does not include a tool the user needs. Furthermore, proprietary software such as Microsoft Office has been improved over the course of many years and may offer more features than do customizable counterparts.

Many users are simply more familiar with proprietary software. Microsoft Word is a clear example of this, as many users learned word processing with this program. Furthermore, since its first release in 1983, Microsoft Word has been written for the most popular platforms in personal computing, including the IBM PC, Apple's Macintosh, and Microsoft Windows.

What is undeniable and of central interest here is the way that an open source project like Mozilla—and specifically one of Mozilla's scope and longevity—fosters civic engagement and participation. For Mozilla, participation is the goal. Open source is a tool to engender that participation.

Recursive Publics

Netscape's premise in publishing its source code and making it available for enhancement (under the terms of an open source license) by *qualified* individuals was that such an arrangement would solicit the expertise of an effectively unlimited pool of programmers in the development of future releases of the Netscape browser.[11] Individuals would qualify themselves to revise the source code on the basis of their enthusiasm, their ability to identify an aspect of the code base that needed improvement, their ability to execute that improvement, and their willingness to submit their work to a vetting process that can be described as distributed peer review. On one hand, Netscape's use of *crowdsourcing* gave it the ability to recruit individual talent, and on the other hand to create an online—and thus geographically unlimited—network of programmers. Volunteers who were professionally or by avocation skilled software developers were invited not only to contribute their expertise, but also to publicly or anonymously affiliate themselves with what Christopher M. Kelty terms a "recursive public":

A recursive public is a public that is vitally concerned with the material and practical maintenance and modification of the technical, legal, practical, and conceptual means of its own existence as a public; it is a collective independent of other forms of constituted power and is capable of speaking to existing forms of power through the production of actually existing alternatives. Free Software is one instance of this concept. . . . Recursive publics, and publics generally, differ from interest groups, corporations, unions, professions, churches, and other forms of organization because of their focus on the radical technological modifiability of their own terms of existence.[12]

In seeking to identify its public by offering a sense of itself as a community, Netscape was engendering a movement dedicated to the common cause of software use and development. The delineation of this public required source code visibility, a quality comparable in political theory to *transparency*, and a shared sense of mission. Participants needed to believe that they were more than free labor and to trust that their contributions were not pro forma, but would be taken seriously. Netscape needed to avoid creating a project that only seemed to invite collaboration. Again, Kelty:

In any public there inevitably arises a moment when the question of how things are said, who controls the means of communication, or whether each and everyone is being properly heard becomes an issue. A legitimate public sphere is one that gives outsiders a way in: they may or may not be heard, but they do not have to appeal to any authority (inside or outside the organization) in order to have a voice. Such publics are not inherently modifiable, but are made so—and maintained— through the practices of participants.[13]

How Mozilla governs volunteer participation toward the end of creating a "legitimate public sphere . . . that gives outsiders a way in" will be explored in some detail in upcoming sections. But first we start by explaining the initial online structure—the tools and the governance—that makes participation possible in the first place.

As of March 31, 1998, developers from around the world could download and modify the nearly eight megabytes of Communicator 5.0 code from mozilla.org, the Web site for the

Mozilla Organization. Founded largely by Netscape employees who were working independently of Netscape, the Mozilla Organization was created as an open source enterprise to coordinate testing of the first Mozilla browser. (Then synonymous with the Web site, mozilla.org, the Mozilla Organization became the Mozilla Foundation in 2003 under the same URL. In accordance with the nomenclature currently published at mozilla. org, we may refer collectively to the ongoing open source projects facilitated at the Web site as the Mozilla Project. Established with financial assistance from Netscape's parent company, AOL, the Mozilla Foundation is the independent, nonprofit organization that oversees the open source Mozilla Project. Since the Mozilla Project's inception as the Mozilla Organization in 1998, the Web browser known today as Firefox has gone through several incarnations—iterations, generations, releases—each of them developed as open source projects.)

To this day, the Mozilla Project hosts the process for facilitating input from volunteer programmers in the maintenance and improvement of the Firefox browser at mozilla.org. Based on a system of distributed decision making, this Web site manages the interactions between developers and Mozilla principals. It also houses the Mozilla Concurrent Versions System (CVS) source repository. Known more generically as a Version Control System, CVS is a free software control system released under the GNU GPL that, by keeping track of all work underway in the development of the code base, enables remote, asynchronous collaboration among developers. As with a lending library, developers "check out" files and ultimately publish their revisions—"check-ins"—in the repository. The CVS source repository is a public resource.[14] Other Version Control Systems that are applied to collaboration in nonprogramming enterprises at Mozilla are also treated as public resources.

While the Internet enables geographically distributed communities to cohere around a common cause or interest, structure is necessary for people working across a distance to become a community. Mozilla.org facilitates such a community. As one of many tools available to the general public at Mozilla.org, the Mozilla Version Control Systems provide the necessary technological architecture to support the community in its distributed work. Having a well-designed system by which individuals can contribute to the shared work of the group is essential to forging a recursive public. Without the ability to manage volunteer contributions quickly and cheaply, the sponsor organization can ill afford to support public participation. Experts and enthusiasts can ill afford to join a community without the mechanism to take effective action together. In addition to the tools, the organization has to be committed to the notion of crowdsourced participation. Without that, it will not publicize its needs, invite engagement, and ultimately communicate the ways in which those outside its boundaries can help. Mozilla's beginnings are rooted in both the culture and practices of open and collaborative work.

The Scope of Participation

Most software users are not programmers and do not seek software the way hobbyists from earlier generations purchased Heathkits to build their own shortwave radios. Software users want their browser to work. They want bug-free software that offers them the tools they need to maximize their personal-computing capabilities. If the number of people willing to volunteer their time and expertise to open-source software development is miniscule compared to the total number of people who use the software, the population willing to work together as a part of a group is even more limited, calling into question the scope of a community required to develop code and the tradeoffs implicit in this style of participation.

In a 2008 interview at Stanford University, the chairman of the Mozilla Foundation, Mitchell Baker, talked about participation rates in any given project:

> The number of people who participate may be small. The important thing is that when there is an issue you care about—and there may be only one or two issues that matter to you. The important thing is that you have the opportunity to participate. You have the option to be more than a consumer. You can create something when you need it. Most of the time, most of us won't want to participate. Not everyone is involved all the time. But the option to get involved is fundamental. What's important to us is that we have enough people getting involved when something is wrong.[15]

Despite the unquestionable success of Mozilla at crowdsourcing experts from around the world, in a public dedicated to any one project under the Mozilla banner, recursive means *rarified*. As with *Wikipedia*, where a far smaller number than the actual visitor count writes the encyclopedia entries, Mozilla attracts a small number of volunteer developers relative to the overall number of people using its software. Ohloh.com, a Web site designed as a directory of open source projects, lists 152 developers who have contributed nearly 7,000 "commits" to the Firefox browser under the GNU General Public License 2.0,

GNU Lesser General Public License 2.1, and Mozilla Public License 1.1.[16] This is not quite an accurate headcount, however, as this figure accounts only for "front-end" coders—programmers who design the user interface. Ohloh.com identifies an additional 824 programmers who work on the "back end"— software that performs the final stage of a process and may not be apparent to the user. A short list of additional Firefox-related projects—Mozilla Chrome, SpiderMonkey, Fennec, and Firebug—accounts for a couple of hundred more programmers. Taking into consideration that many programmers work on more than one project, we estimate that one thousand individual programmers help to develop and maintain the Firefox browser, now used by an estimated 270 million people.[17] These numbers may not be historically accurate, but they probably reflect the general ratio of programmers to end-users.

When in the late 1990s Netscape published the Communicator source code, one of the more compelling critiques of open source centered on the administrative challenge of incorporating what could become *too much* input (from too many participants) in decision-making processes that traditionally turn on the decisions of an individual or a relatively small group of managers. In his book *The Success of Open Source*, Steven Weber recalls the idiom of "having too many cooks in the kitchen":[18]

The dilemmas are familiar. Monitoring and evaluating the performance of a complex task like writing code is expensive and imperfect. Proxy measures of achievement are hard to come by. Quality is as important (often more important) than quantity, and simple measures are likely to be as misleading as informative (someone who produces a large number of lines of code may be demonstrating poor implementation skills, not productivity). Shirking within teams and free riding on the efforts of others is hard to isolate. One person's good efforts can be rendered ineffective by another person's failure to produce.

With this passage, Weber is introducing a well-known principle-cum-proverb from the literature of software engineering known as Brook's Law: "Adding manpower to a late software project makes it later."[19] In other words, the overall productivity of a team is diminished while added experts come up to speed on a project. Fred Brooks, a manager of IBM's OS/360 project, called this the "ramp up" time. He argued that the number of bugs created increases exponentially with the number of people added to a team.

Weber and other writers like Eric S. Raymond point out that Brook's Law is not applicable to open-source software development because participants *self-select* to work on a specific project.[20] As Weber further explains, the concept of self-selection invites individuals to nominate themselves for participation in a project of their own choosing:

The key element of the open source process, as an ideal type, is voluntary participation and voluntary selection of tasks. Anyone can join an open source project, and anyone can leave at any time. That is not just a free market in labor. What makes it different from the theoretical option of exit from a corporate organization is this: Each person is free to choose what he wishes to work on or to contribute. There is no consciously organized or enforced division of labor. In fact the underlying notion of a division of labor doesn't fit the open source process at all. Labor is *distributed*, certainly—it could hardly be otherwise in projects that involve large numbers of contributors. But it is not really divided in the industrial sense of the term.[21]

Thus, the volunteer open-source code developer completes her selected task on her own time, prior to review, without the guarantee that her contribution will be implemented. She works on spec. The only guarantee granted the volunteer is that her proposed contribution, submitted via a clear and public protocol, will be taken seriously. It is also significant that Weber is describing the open source process as "an ideal type."

Because the utility of the volunteer developer's code modification—known colloquially as a *patch*—determines the applicability of her patch to the project at hand, the proliferation of bugs that Brooks associates with the increase in personnel is checked. As we will see in the case of Mozilla, volunteers submit their patches to a system of distributed peer review. Self-selection is the starting point of that process. As such, the peer review of patches from volunteer developers serves to initiate *individuals* new to the Mozilla community on the basis of their technical knowledge.

Self-selection engenders another aspect of quality control in open-source software development, one based not on the expertise of the individual developer, but on the *collective* ability of developers to scrutinize code, as summarized in Raymond's articulation of Linus's Law: "Given a large enough beta-tester and co-developer base, almost every problem will be characterized quickly and the fix will be obvious to someone." Raymond also states the same idea less formally: "Given enough eyeballs, all bugs are shallow."[22]

Of course, all programmers are not looking at the same piece of code. An open source process works best if the overall project or objective of the organization is modular; each module can benefit from specialization on the part of the individuals who comprise the recursive public.

A key characteristic of the Firefox browser is that source code is often *modular*. Modularity promotes specialization and the concept of comparative advantage between individuals in a recursive public. Modularity arguably is part of the open source definition because the organization of source files into chunks within a software program isolates tasks on the basis of functionality. A volunteer developer dedicates himself to the specific fix he deems necessary within the parameters set by the module. He chooses a topic he is most qualified to work on. Because modularity dedicates the programmer to a single component of the code base, it is the basis for specifying, soliciting, and organizing contributions from volunteers.

Finally, it is noteworthy that the *ideal* open source process that includes such concepts and practices as self-selection, peer review, and modularity may or may not identify an open source operation's management style as top-down or by degrees more bottom-up. As we will describe in subsequent sections, the Mozilla model relies on leadership to steer the process. Asa Dotzler, Director of Community Development at the Mozilla Corporation, a taxable subsidiary of the Mozilla Foundation, explains that programmers are encouraged to submit patches for possible implementation, "but management often decides what it wants. Management may recruit programmers from the community to work on specific, underrepresented projects."[23] As such—and as we will explore in greater detail—Mozilla is an example of an open source project that is mediated by managers—a mix of Mozilla employees and prominent volunteers.

In sum, self-selection is the first step in a system of peer review. Self-selection also makes possible the formation of a large group of individuals qualified to work on a specific problem. Regardless of any one developer's standing in the community, a group of self-selected individuals is better suited to track down bugs more efficiently than an individual or a static team of individuals employed by a company dedicated to the development of proprietary software. It is also important to recall Mitchell Baker's observation that not everyone is involved all the time. Participants choose the levels of their involvement. Furthermore, they may vary their involvement as they become familiar with the community. In addition to periodically writing code, a volunteer may also *report* bugs and *propose* "check-ins" to the code repository that he is not capable of addressing with a patch. As such, meaningful distinctions between users and developers begin to diminish, especially when, later in this report, we consider the contributions of users who are not programmers, but who nonetheless contribute to quality assurance and the promotion of the software.

These are several "take-away" lessons of Mozilla's crowdsourcing technique that can be applied more generally to other forms of shared work:

- The ratio of active participants to the total population of a community may be small.
- Individuals must know they have the option to participate.
- Not everyone needs to be involved all the time.
- Participants choose their tasks.
- Participants may discover new roles as they acclimate to the community.
- Leadership may steer participation toward select projects.

Why Software Developers Participate in Open Source

To question why software developers participate in open source foreshadows our inquiry into what would inspire private citizens with technical and nontechnical expertise to contribute to the work of government agencies. In a study conducted by Paul A. David and Joseph S. Shapiro, 1,459 software developers were asked what motivated them to volunteer their time and expertise to open source projects.[24] In the spirit of the ideology of the earliest proponents of the Free Software Movement, nearly 80 percent responded that users "should be free to modify software [they] use." To couple this motivation with the next most often-cited reason for participation, the desire to "give back to community," is to combine a sense of individual rights with the importance of exercising those rights to enhance the prosperity of that community. Pairings of other motivations create similar dichotomies: open-source software development is the "best way for software to be developed," and also a good "way for [the developer] to become a better programmer." Other motivations for participation (in decreasing order of importance) include to:[25]

- Provide alternatives to proprietary software.
- Interact with like-minded programmers.
- Modify existing software as needed.
- Fix bugs in existing software.
- Learn how a particular program works.
- Fulfill an employer's stipulation for the programmer to collaborate in open source projects.

David and Shapiro also compare developers' motivations for choosing their first open source projects with those for participating in subsequent projects. Here, the predominant rationale centered on individual enrichment: the software being developed was technically interesting and would be useful to that particular developer. Still, the importance and visibility of the project itself was a major factor in developers' decisions to join open source projects.

The Mozilla Project confirms these findings. Among software developers and (as we will see) less technically inclined individuals, there is a desire to participate, if given the opportunity. Where participation is mutually beneficial to the organization, the volunteer, and the volunteer's community, there is a greater likelihood of engagement.

The Mozilla Manifesto

In light of the advantages and disadvantages of open source, community-based coding involves a set of practices, both ideological and commercial, that has quickly become a permanent aspect of the software industry. With the example of the Firefox browser, the input of a proportionately small, self-selected group of programmers must address the needs of a user base outside the technically savvy core of users if the Mozilla Foundation is to build market share while simultaneously educating the general public about its core mission. This mission, which we quote at length here, was published as "The Mozilla Manifesto" in 2007, and illustrates the intersection of individual rights with the antiproprietary activism of open source in the maintenance of the Internet as a social sphere, where the Internet itself is a public resource:

1. The Internet is an integral part of modern life—a key component in education, communication, collaboration, business, entertainment, and society as a whole.

2. The Internet is a global public resource that must remain open and accessible.

3. The Internet should enrich the lives of individual human beings.

4. Individuals' security on the Internet is fundamental and cannot be treated as optional.

5. Individuals must have the ability to shape their own experiences on the Internet.

6. The effectiveness of the Internet as a public resource depends upon interoperability (protocols, data formats, content), innovation, and decentralized participation worldwide.

7. Free and open source software promotes the development of the Internet as a public resource.

8. Transparent community-based processes promote participation, accountability, and trust.

9. Commercial involvement in the development of the Internet brings many benefits; a balance between commercial goals and public benefit is critical.

10. Magnifying the public-benefit aspects of the Internet is an important goal, worthy of time, attention, and commitment.[26]

Open Source at Mozilla

Introduction

The independent Mozilla Organization was born in the late 1990s, at the apogee of the Silicon Valley dot-com boom. Even the proponents of free software who were nonetheless skeptical of the application of free-software doctrine to commercial interests saw the release of Communicator source code, the quickening of new projects under open source licenses, and the spinoff of the Mozilla Organization as allied with the intentions of a grassroots movement that began in the 1960s.

Today, the Mozilla Project is building a recursive public, a *constituency* dedicated to the improvement and distribution of Mozilla products via the Internet. Individuals volunteer their time and expertise to the Mozilla Project because the Internet is essential to their daily lives. They participate because they have identified a reason to do so, and because they can: Mozilla provides online, group-based structures for collaboration. These generalizations foresee the potential of similar models of participation to link private citizens to decision-making processes within government.

One way to begin understanding the relevance of the Mozilla Project to emerging forms of collaborative governance is to note that Mozilla's reason for existing is not solely to distribute products. In its manifesto, the Mozilla Project abstractly identifies the Internet as "an integral part of modern life." Slightly more concrete, the Internet is "a global public resource," one promoted by free and open source processes. If we combine the idea of the Internet as a public resource with another tenet in the Mozilla manifesto—that "individuals must have the ability to shape their own experiences on the Internet"—a portable picture of participation begins to emerge. We can see the end-user *advocating* the terms of her continued participation in the maintenance of the Internet as a public resource via her own input in the improvement of the products that enable her online experience.

Applied to technical and nontechnical enterprises, an open source process may influence the development, distribution, and ongoing improvement of products and services that are collaborative in nature. If for instance a potential participant in open-source software development is physically impaired *and* skilled in programming, he may by dint of his personal experiences and technical expertise self-select himself to collaborate in the creation of software that limits the number of keystrokes required for him to access resources on the Internet. We may modify this example in anticipation of our discussion on nontechnical input from participants in the Mozilla experience by imagining the same participant, physically impaired but in this case nontechnical in his avocation or vocation. If he has a vested interest in online services, he may still contribute his input to an organization like Mozilla if a structure is in place to receive it. He may describe the limitations his disability places on his access to the Internet. In fact, some of the strides that Mozilla has made in increasing Internet accessibility for the visually- and mobility-impaired were born from the input of volunteers and organizations historically unaffiliated with Mozilla.[27]

In another example that comingles browser design and the inherent skills of browser-users, when version 3.5 of the Firefox browser was released in June of 2009, it shipped in over 70 languages; the development of these foreign-language versions of the browser was volunteer-based.[28]

One final way to introduce the parallels between open source and collaborative governance is to recall common rulemaking procedures that traditionally give private citizens a voice in government. Passed into law in 1946, the Administrative Procedure Act (APA) affords private citizens the right to comment on the specifics of new laws enacted by Congress and the president. As the constituents affected by a new law, individuals are invited to respond to the rules and regulations that interpret the language of that law. Known as Notice and Comment Rulemaking, this period of public comment is inaugurated with the publication of the new law (as a "notice of proposed rulemaking" [NPRM]) in the *Federal Register*, and generally remains open for between 30 and one 180 days.

Though the comparison between open-source software development and Notice and Comment Rulemaking is abstract at this juncture, several commonalities between these enterprises prefigure our discussion of collaborative governance:

• New laws and software modules are published and made available for public review.

• Both enterprises determine the nature of the feedback they are seeking. Both set the agenda.

• Participants offer feedback on a voluntary basis.

• Public feedback is garnered for set periods of time; in the case of open source software, code modifications are subject to deadlines, as predicated by project timelines.

• Just as self-selecting software developers are experts in their field, individuals who respond to NPRMs are commonly self-selecting because their professions or private lives will be impacted by the new law. Or they are experts summoned by governmental agencies because they can contribute scientific- or industry-specific expertise crucial to the wording of the rules and regulations under review.

Though this list is more suggestive than exhaustive, it articulates an *ideal* with regard to the potential not only for an organization to tailor products and/or policies to the needs of constituencies, but also for individuals to respond to policies of governing that most impact their daily lives. Of these policies, which would each of them be most qualified to work on, based on personal experience and enthusiasm? And if qualified to do so, how will they provide useful feedback to policy makers—their representatives—in government?

In this section our focus is on software development. Here, in anticipation of our expanding discussion of the potential influence of open source software on open government, we introduce a contemporary culture of collaboration between volunteer software developers and the Mozilla Foundation. In describing the protocols by which the Mozilla Foundation solicits expertise from the public in the management of the Firefox browser, we present a system of governance best described as a *hierarchical meritocracy*. We begin with an explanation of the practice of distributed decision making, and its attendant system of distributed peer review.

Module Owners and Their Peers

Distributed decision making, a concept well documented by organizational and industrial psychologists, refers to a work environment in which "decision making is a continuous, interpersonal process, usually involving several 'decision makers' aiming at dynamic and cooperative control of the state of affairs at work."[29] Specific to the Mozilla Foundation and its appropriation of this concept, an introduction to aspiring hackers at mozilla.org states the following:

The Mozilla project is far too big for any one person—or even a small set of people—to make ongoing decisions regarding code appropriateness, quality, or readiness to be checked into the CVS source repository. . . . The code is large and complex; the number of daily decisions to be made is enormous. The project would slow to a crawl if a small set of people tried to make the majority of decisions regarding particular pieces of code.[30]

This statement is the opening remark in a primer entitled "Distributed Decision-Making: Mozilla Modules and Module Ownership," which describes the role of the module owner in the production of the Firefox browser. A module owner leads the development of a module of code. A code module is a collection of related source files. "Modules are chunks of code," explains Mitchell Baker, "and there are quite a number of them. The module owner is responsible for that area, that module; no change is made without her or his okay. You need prior review."[31]

The module owner designates peers to help him determine the utility of patches. Peers are developers with a proven track record from within the Mozilla community. Together with his peers, the module owner makes final decisions about modifications of the module he oversees.

Committers

A developer who successfully submits a patch to a code module associated with the Firefox browser is known as a committer. A committer receives permission from a module owner to modify its source code. If a potential committer is not one of the original developers of the Firefox browser, he seeks approval from established committers in the Mozilla community. "If you want to participate," explains Baker, "you can't put the code into the tree. There's another layer, called a committer. Before you're allowed to combine your work in the public asset, Mozilla needs to know you. Mozilla needs to be comfortable with your work."[32]

To become a committer, a volunteer developer begins by finding a project to work on and, after talking with established developers in Mozilla's programming community, submits a formal application to become a committer. While becoming active in the Mozilla community by contributing to the online dialog at mozilla.org and joining mailing lists, the aspiring committer next submits a patch to a code module for review. He does so by nominating potential peers to "vouch" for his proposed patch. These individuals—awkwardly termed "vouchers"—act as mentors to the volunteer and, accordingly, assume responsibility for the newcomer's patch. If the volunteer's formal application is approved and his patch is proven effective, he becomes a committer. He has established relationships with active committers and module owners, who "vouch" for him as an expert, and he is granted "commit privileges" by the virtual management team at Mozilla. If he decides to continue with Mozilla as a committer, he may make a formal application to become a "voucher" or peer to incoming volunteers. He may also ascend to the role of module owner—an individual who manages the maintenance and development of a specific module in the Firefox code tree.

It is important to note that when occasionally Mozilla pays a developer to work on a specific module, that developer matriculates via the same process as a volunteer.[33]

In sum, individual recognition and advancement in the community-based production of software at Mozilla is a meritocracy, predicated on the utility of the developer's contributions and his resultant visibility and effectiveness within the online community. Brian Behlendorf, a founding member of the Apache Software Foundation and a board member of the Mozilla Foundation explains that the standing of a developer in the Mozilla community is formed on the basis of "the assignment of capabilities to various people, such as those with 'commit privileges.' If you've been awarded those, that can carry some moral weight when having a conversation; [A] sense of who someone is, is based on [his] informal reputation in the community, his track record of contributions, that sort of thing."[34]

In an earlier section we noted that Mozilla leadership might actively steer programmers toward underrepresented projects. As we will see in greater detail in subsequent sections, this concept of oversight cannot be stressed enough in differentiating Mozilla's open source approach from other contemporary examples of crowdsourcing. Unlike entries published in the online encyclopedia *Wikipedia*, peer review of new code dedicated to developing Mozilla products happens before that code is implemented. Mozilla does not publish works-in-progress. In this way, Mozilla combines the knowledge base inherent in a self-selecting crowd of experts with the kind of leadership that defines a representative democracy.

Mozilla's Module Ownership System

Despite the word-of-mouth—and as such, *social*—nature of individual advancement in the Mozilla community, the Mozilla Foundation has published a specific protocol by which developers are qualified as committers.[35] Once an individual achieves committer status, she may join the virtual management team at Mozilla not only as a module owner, but also as a super-reviewer or a release driver.[36] A brief description of these roles further illustrates the application of distributed decision making to the production of software at Mozilla.

To summarize this process, we begin with the volunteer developer: she identifies a bug in a module—a problem she wants to work on. She submits her bug fix at mozilla.org with her application to become a committer. An established committer acts as her voucher. This voucher often solicits the backing of a second voucher to determine whether or not the submitted bug fix requires super-review. Super-reviewers differ from module owners in that they scrutinize patches on the basis of the interoperability of code modules. Super-reviewers are good at integrating modules. They conduct what we may accurately term *integration review*.[37]

Whereas committers submit patches to Mozilla in response to their specific software needs as users of the Firefox browser, release drivers (another managerial role) steer developers toward bug fixes in anticipation of what Mozilla calls "milestone" software releases.[38] In contrast with module owners and super-reviewers, release drivers do not focus on the specific technical advances in source code; instead, they oversee management of the source tree in the time leading up to the release of a new version of a software application. Release drivers participate seasonally in the development of the Firefox browser. They are thought leaders and innovators from within Mozilla and also from the software industry at large—from universities and such companies as IBM and Red Hat—who periodically volunteer their time, enthusiasm, and expertise to particular projects.

The Governance Module

The module ownership system is mirrored in nontechnical projects with the creation of so-called activities modules. Each activities module has an owner, at least one peer reviewer (and often more than one), a volunteer newsgroup dedicated to the collection and dissemination of information about module activities, and a specific list of responsibilities. Examples include the governance module, which is a module dedicated to the administration—staffing, scheduling, conflict resolution—of code modules, and Planet Mozilla, which is the module that, comparable to a virtual press office, maintains Mozilla's image in the blogosphere. (Planet Mozilla is a Web site that syndicates blogs devoted to the Mozilla Project.[39] The Planet Mozilla module owner and his peers are responsible for determining not only which blogs will be included at planet.mozilla.org, but also what content from selected blogs will be published.)

The governance module is broadly responsible for the processes by which the Mozilla Foundation distributes decision making. Though the governance module owner and her peers are not necessarily software developers, their management extends to oversight of the source code repository.

There are also submodules that manage governance functions. One fills vacancies on existing projects, staffs new modules, reviews the performance of module owners, and resolves conflicts involving module owners, peers, and contributing developers. Another governance submodule manages incubator repositories, which are temporary source code repositories for volunteer developers who are seeking commit privileges but are not yet well known in the Mozilla development community. Such repositories help educate new participants.

A Hierarchical Meritocracy

We have already suggested the power of both crowdsourcing and the oversight described by Linus's Law to source and utilize expertise. Self-selection means that everyone is invited to contribute his time and expertise to the development of the Firefox browser. Individuals who make useful contributions to the Mozilla Project, and who demonstrate their desire to take on greater responsibilities within the virtual community by becoming increasingly involved in the online *culture* of Mozilla, gain prestige in the Mozilla development community. They may choose—and be chosen to—take on a managerial role. Despite the centrality of volunteer peer review in this process, module owners make final decisions. Most are volunteers. As such, the module ownership system is democratic, but also hierarchical and meritocratic at the same time.

Delegation of authority not only expands the knowledge base of the delegator—in this case, the module owner—but also distributes ownership of the consequences of final decisions. Delegation also increases the sense of belonging on the part of the individual who, on the basis of her abilities, has been given authority.

Despite these benefits, a manager's delegation of responsibilities to individuals in a group does not necessarily enable that group to make a collaborative decision. What makes participation in the maintenance of a code module collaborative is a developer's sense of autonomy, in combination with a shared sense of mission. She is autonomous in that she writes code in response to her personal experiences with the software. She is a collaborator because she submits her patch to a group of peers for review and possible implementation. And she is invited to choose what she wants to do.

Licensing

Introduction

Essential to the success of the Mozilla Project today is Netscape's historic decision to license the browser software to the public under an open source license. Communicator source code was released in 1998 under "Project Source 331." This project marked Netscape's effort to release open source code to the public and resulted in the Netscape Public License (NPL), which became the Mozilla Public License (MPL). While GNU used the General Public License (GPL) to guard against businesses co-opting open source code for their own private benefit, the Mozilla Foundation licenses the Firefox browser source code under one of three open source licenses designed to encourage innovation while maintaining the integrity of the Mozilla brand. They are the Mozilla Public License, the GNU General Public License, and the GNU Lesser General Public License. Our focus on the MPL illustrates how licenses govern the redistribution of work by volunteers, while at the same time promoting participation. We conclude this section with the presentation of two definitive features of open source software: forking and portability.

The Mozilla Public License

Like a constitution, a license is a set of rules that governs the rights of use, in this case with regard to the terms under which a programmer modifies code for distribution by Mozilla *and* himself, when his contributions are applied to other programs. There are many different kinds of licenses. Many organizations have developed licenses appropriate to their products and ideologies of distribution. From the point of view of the licensee, an open source license enables him to:

- Use open source software for any purpose whatsoever.
- Make copies of open source software and to distribute them without payment of royalties to a licensor.
- Create derivative works of open source software and to distribute them without payment of royalties to a licensor.
- Access and use the source code of open source software.
- Combine open source and other software.

The main question facing the licensee concerns how much he needs to contribute to the community. How much can he go off on his own? Open source is software that is available to anyone free of charge. Nevertheless, at Mozilla, if you improve software you have to make that improvement available to everyone, and have a social incentive to do so. This does not mean that a licensee necessarily has to publish at mozilla.org.

But he does have to make his modification available under the same license that granted him source code use in the first place.

The MPL creates recursion. Its reciprocity provisions create *return* and an incentive to participate as a member of the community. If a licensee modifies and distributes a file containing either the original source code or a prior modification to the original code, he must distribute his modification under the MPL. The licensee is permitted to use all prior modifications of the source code; at the same time, he is permitting future modification of his contribution.

Firefox as a Project Fork

In the late 1990s, the Mozilla Organization took over the development and management of the source code for the Netscape Communicator browser, which included the Netscape Navigator browser. The Mozilla Organization was in operation from 1998 to 2003, when it became the independent Mozilla Foundation. Today, the Foundation, which is synonymous with the Mozilla Project, owns the intellectual property (trademarks, brands, logos) and infrastructure (servers) related to Mozilla. Contributors keep copyright to their additions. This is the covenant between Mozilla and its contributors: copyright is ownership.

The creation of the Firefox browser under the management of the Mozilla Organization illustrates an essential aspect of open source coding. In 1998, one of the challenges Netscape faced was the right of an individual to apply her contribution to the Mozilla source code to the founding of a new project. The big question: To what extent did Netscape need to guard against other businesses co-opting—or "forking"—its open source code for their own private benefit?

In software engineering, a project fork occurs when programmers base their development of a new software package on the source code of existing software. Open source software may be forked without permission.[40] Accordingly, forks can be sanctioned—"friendly forks"—or hostile. One of the essential advantages of forking is that it allows for and invites experimentation and innovation. The entire module ownership system at Mozilla is predicated on the fecundity of sanctioned forking. Sanctioned forking expands community by simultaneously increasing the number of participants and, by way of their participation, deepening the knowledge base of the community. The possibility that a programmer could appropriate Mozilla source code and then, after collaborating with the development community, abandon Mozilla necessitates a hierarchical and formal process of gaining commit privileges, as summarized earlier in this report. In short, the threat of a hostile fork requires strong leadership on the part of Mozilla and a public commitment to the Mozilla community on the part of the contributor.

The Firefox browser is itself the result of a sanctioned fork. The Mozilla Organization began development of what would become Firefox under the name Phoenix. Phoenix became the Firebird project, before the Firefox browser, a project launched as an experimental alternative to the Mozilla Suite, emerged as the main product of the newly formed Mozilla Foundation. As a free and open source Web browser, Firefox has consistently gained market share since its debut in November 2004. Each incarnation of what became the Firefox browser was developed by a community of individual programmers extending beyond the employees of Netscape and Mozilla.

Bugzilla: An Example of Portability

A final role available to volunteer developers—one similar to the module owner—is that of the Bugzilla component owner. Bugzilla is an online, open-source bug-tracking system that merits mention because it is a profound example of *portability*, an aspect of open source that is conversely related to the practice of forking. To port software is to use it without modification, but to apply it to platforms for which it was not originally intended. Portability means that innovations can be adopted for unforeseen uses.

Licensed under the MPL, Bugzilla is like the Mozilla source code repository in that it too is a Version Control System (VCS). Designed by Netscape and launched in tandem with mozilla.org in 1998 via an anonymous VCS, Bugzilla allows registered users to report bugs encountered in their use of the Firefox browser and other software. Because the system is licensed under the MPL, it is portable: an organization other than Mozilla can adapt the system to any open source or proprietary platform free of charge, instead of creating a fork. Portability suggests the potential reach of open source software into the technological infrastructures of NGOs and governmental agencies alike, a potential supported by the fact that over eight hundred organizations are known to use Bugzilla, though the number may be much higher. These organizations include free software projects such as Gnome, the Apache Project, and Open Office; Linux distributions such as Red Hat and Novell; and companies like Facebook, the New York Times, and NASA.[41]

This is the paradox of open source. The license creates the freedom to splinter off and develop new projects, while the peer production of distributed work creates the incentive to collaborate as a community. Anticipating the optimal level of forking versus coming together that will produce innovation is the key to success.

In conclusion, the Mozilla Public License is one component of the shared responsibility of transparency and collaborative governance. A viral license mandates that collaboration and transparency are repeatable and repeated. But the open source license is not sufficient. The license is the set of rules under which community norms are practiced and proliferate over time. Transparency requires vigilance on the part of the principals at Mozilla and, in the context of software, the programming community at large. As we have seen, this vigilance is made possible by the online infrastructure of the open source process.

Beyond Software

Introduction

Some facets of the Mozilla Project are not concerned with source code development, but nevertheless are organized as modules. Module owners in nontechnical areas seek experts in marketing, user support, beta testing, and event planning. Nontechnical modules are hierarchical in nature; Mozilla collaborates with individuals who are on paths to leadership roles in the Mozilla Project.

Mozilla crowdsources technical support for Firefox users at support.mozilla.com, a Web site known by its acronym, SUMO (SUpport.MOzilla.com).[42] SUMO is a portal to a suite of social networking tools that enable Firefox users to seek technical advice from each other in a variety of formats. Mozilla also uses the Internet to organize a global network of user groups. These groups promote the Firefox browser by performing such business practices as public relations and research and development on a grassroots level. Commensurate with a regional sales force, user groups also advocate the use of the Firefox browser in their local communities.

Volunteer User Support

The widespread use of social networking tools such as electronic mailing lists (listserv), wikis, online chat rooms, and blogs, and the rise in popularity of social networking services like MySpace and Facebook beyond the presence and scope of even the most enduring fads, suggest the potential of the interconnectedness of communications technologies to create more and vaster online communities. The use of a Web site as a portal to an aggregation of networks demonstrates a basic design principle in the interdependence of online media. Single Web sites often link to blogs, chat rooms, services such as Facebook, and other Web sites. The Mozilla Foundation consolidates its online reach at mozilla.org, "an entry point that provides a high-level overview of the different community areas."[43]

Firefox users access technical support at the SUMO Web site.[44] Navigating SUMO, individuals can either seek technical advice or volunteer their knowledge of the browser to the troubleshooting of technical problems faced by online peers. Community-based support at SUMO takes three forms: wiki, blog, and chat room.

The SUMO Knowledge Base is a collection of articles written by and for Firefox users on basic troubleshooting, browser installation procedures, browser customization through add-ons, data recovery, and many other topics. Browser users are also invited to edit and update articles. They translate postings into other languages. In the spirit of *Wikipedia*, the Knowledge Base is a continuously updated, community-written user manual. New articles and editorial changes to existing articles are approved and published in the Knowledge Base through a managerial system similar to module ownership.[45] A new or revised article is placed in a staging area for review by the online community. Contributors with "approver" authority act as the contributing writer's peer reviewers. They approve articles and transfer them in the Knowledge Base.

The Knowledge Base is the first tier in what Mozilla stakeholders call the "support funnel"—a series of volunteer-based SUMO resources that helps the user find answers to his questions about Firefox.[46] If an individual does not find the solution to his problem in the Knowledge Base, he may direct his questions to a support forum, of which there are many in the online Mozilla community. Support forums are blogs linked to support.mozilla. com. An individual begins by browsing the blog directories to see if the community has already addressed his topic of interest. If not, he is free to post a new question and introduce a new thread. As with the Knowledge Base, support forums are maintained by volunteers and depend on a culture of peer review.

One may also seek technical advice in a chat room at support. mozilla.com. These forums are similar to the blog-based forums, except that conversation between the inquirer and the volunteer expert is live.

Some instructive qualities of SUMO that may be applied to governance include the following:

- Participants can document their experiences.
- By publishing their accounts online, participants can contribute to a community-wide knowledge base, one that can be organized by issue.

- Networked governance may be organized with Web pages.
- A Web page may serve as a portal to other online resources in other formats.

Firefox User Groups

The Mozilla development community is bound by the tenets articulated in the Mozilla Manifesto, one of which states that "[t]he effectiveness of the Internet as a public resource depends upon interoperability (protocols, data formats, content), innovation and decentralized participation worldwide."[47] Decentralized participation on the scale achieved by Mozilla would be unimaginable without the Internet. Firefox users from around the world contribute to the promotion of the browser by forming or joining online user groups or both. As such, Mozilla is more than an open source developer of software: Mozilla applies the concept of community-based software development to *open source marketing*. Individuals join user groups at spreadfirefox.com, a link at mozilla.org. There are over 200 user groups in this online directory.

Open Source Marketing

Many user groups have only a few members. Others, like FoxieWire, a news site dedicated to "everything Mozilla," have nearly 10,000 members.[48] It serves Mozilla as a volunteer press corps, posting to a communal blog any news items about Firefox, the Thunderbird mail server, and Firefox add-ons. Though it is difficult to ascertain how many of these members are actively posting news items at any given time, foxiewire. com had on average an estimated 12,000 unique visitors each month in 2008. They made an average of 18,000 visits to the site per month.[49] A far smaller number of people contribute to FoxieWire than visit the site for information. Everyone who does contribute postings is a volunteer.

FoxieWire recalls the history of the Associated Press (AP), a cooperative owned by its contributing news agencies. Like the AP, FoxieWire is subscriber-based, however subscription to it takes the form of free registration as a member. Also similar to the AP, the Mozilla Foundation is a nonprofit organization that operates like a public utility, in that it does not refuse service to anyone who wants to use the browser. FoxieWire echoes the function of news organizations such as Slashdot.com, a technology-related news site featuring contributions by its users.

Similar to FoxieWire, For the Record (FTR), another user group at spreadfirefox.com, was formed to involve as many people as possible in the telling of the Mozilla story:

For the Record (FTR) is a community-driven public relations and press response program that will harness the energy and knowledge of the Mozilla community to 1) catalog all of the online coverage of the Mozilla Project, 2) develop a sustainable team of spokespeople who feel empowered to respond to online coverage, and 3) build a collection of talking points and responses to frequently asked questions.[50]

Both Web sites share the same function and format. They are both blogs maintained by volunteers, who monitor online coverage of the Mozilla Project. FTR has the more express purpose of managing the image of Firefox in the blogosphere by preparing spokespeople with "talking points." In further contrast with

FoxieWire, FTR has attracted only 30 members, accounting for an average of less than two original postings per month since the end of 2007. This does not mean that FTR will not be a successful and active user group in the future. But it does suggest another characteristic of open source: innovation dependent on decentralized participation requires experimentation and, as such, the understanding that any one project may fail.

In describing the challenges to implementing participatory governance, former CIO of the U.S. Department of Transportation Daniel Mintz writes: "The next administration will face two . . . challenges . . . first, how best to build a government organization that can tolerate failure, at least in small doses, and second, how to make a government agency or department organizationally agile."[51] In the spirit of these insights, we may summarize the success of open source marketing as follows:

- Open source promotes experimentation.
- Open source tolerates failure.

Community-based Research and Development

Another marketing arm of the Mozilla Project that is maintained by volunteers is best classified as R&D. Firefox Stats is a user group designed as an open-source marketing agency for the Mozilla Foundation. Its site publishes data about browser market share and links to such blogs as the *Blog of Metrics*, a formal accounting of the browsers used by individuals to download the Firefox browser.[52] Much like news items, raw data as text and graphics are made available for public use. The service mirrors the offerings of a growing number of civic organizations established to make data both available and useable. The Sunlight Foundation promotes transparency in the United States Congress by aggregating information for use by journalists and bloggers.

A Mozilla Sales Force

User groups can also approximate a volunteer sales force. Mozilla Campus Reps is one such group that trains individuals to introduce the Mozilla Project on college campuses.[53] Campus reps in the United States and India post interviews with browser users on YouTube.[54] Campus reps invite students to participate in Mozilla Lab's "Design Challenge," a contest-like forum for students of design to develop software prototypes for the Internet.[55] Mozilla also sponsors contests in the area of marketing at ImpactMozilla.com. Contestants are invited to submit executive summaries of marketing plans aimed at increasing Firefox's user retention.[56]

The use of games and contests by NGOs and government agencies to increase public awareness of their enterprises is not new. The U.S. Fish and Wildlife Service annually hosts the Federal Duck Stamp Contest. The oldest wildlife art contest in the country, it aims to increase public awareness of waterfowl management in North America.

World Without Oil was an alternative-reality game, which meant that participants played the roles of themselves, instead of creating avatars. The object of the game was for each player to submit depictions—blogs, graphics, emails, phone messages—of what their everyday lives would be like without oil. By June of 2007, when the game ended, over 60,000 people from around the world had participated.[57]

Global Promotions

The common interest in promoting Firefox transcends territorial and cultural boundaries. User groups have started up in many countries throughout the world. In his book *Internet Politics: States, Citizens, and New Communication Technologies*, Andrew Chadwick writes:

Participants engaged in online behavior, such as those, for instance, involved in Usernet discussions, may reside anywhere. What brings them together is not their territorial identity . . . but common interests that often transcend national boundaries.[58]

Some of the Firefox user groups, like the group Spread Firefox in Maldives, have only a few members. The group calling itself Spread Firefox in the U.A.E has only 14 members. The groups Farsi Firefox, Firefox 4 Sri Lankans, Firefox @ Argentina, and Firefox Armenia, and groups from Finland, Hong Kong, Greece, Israel, and dozens of other countries, suggest the collective enthusiasm of Firefox users to promote the browser globally. We are reminded of the following points:

- The asset that Mozilla creates is available to the public for use free of charge.
- Mozilla fosters volunteer engagement with its global community through Web sites.

• Having a cause around which people can rally, and for which they can take action, helps to spur engagement.

Mozilla's Use of Social Networking Tools

The global community of Firefox users at spreadfirefox.com has been instrumental in landmark releases of the browser. On June 17, 2008, a day Mozilla dubbed "Download Day," over eight million people downloaded Firefox 3.[59] This set a Guinness World Record for the most downloads in a 24-hour period. By July 2, 2008, over 28 million people had downloaded the newly released version of the Firefox browser. In anticipation of Download Day 2008, Mozilla had distributed badges to user-group Web sites at spreadfirefox.com, at the same time requesting pledges from the groups to download the new browser on Download Day. On that day 43 million people visited spreadfirefox.com.

Spreadfirefox.com and its aggregation of user groups are not wholly responsible for the successful launch of Firefox 3. Mozilla employed social networking services such as Twitter, YouTube, the U.S.-based Facebook, and its Japanese counterparts, Bebo and Mixi, in the promotion of Download Day. Paul Kim, vice president of marketing at Mozilla, explains: "We seeded the [Facebook] community with links of articles and other information that pointed to the Download Day site."[60]

Social networking services allow Mozilla to provide a virtual meeting place for its most avid browser users. In June 2008, the Firefox Facebook fan page listed approximately 115,000 fans. In the same month, unique monthly visitors to social networks like Facebook represented over 60 percent of the world's Internet audience.[61] As of January 2009, Mozilla's Facebook fan base had nearly tripled.[62] Social sites also enable Mozilla to distribute digital information via individual networks of relationships, creating viral channels of distribution.

As we will see in the final section of this report, the success of Mozilla in using the Internet as a medium for collaboration with its browser users suggests the potential of collaboration between governments and constituencies.

Community-based Research and Development Revisited: Mozdev.org

Among the many parallels between Mozilla and collaborative governance that we will explore in the final section of this report is the concept of an NGO acting as a "participation broker" between private citizens and government agencies. In anticipation of—and as an introduction to—this discussion, we look to a similar relationship outside of government. The Mozilla community at large comprises smaller and relatively autonomous communities that recruit experts and enthusiasts for their own sake, with the overall goal of promoting the Mozilla experience. Up to this point we have focused on the ability of the individual to offer her or his expertise to technical and nontechnical projects under the Mozilla banner. Now we begin to shift toward the formation of Mozilla-dedicated groups.

Mozdev.org is a Web site created in 2004 by the Mozdev Community Organization, a nonprofit organization designed to support Mozilla's development community. The author of *Cre-*

ating Applications with Mozilla, a longtime participant in the Mozilla development community, and a principal at Mozdev. org, David Bowell explains:[63]

As the open source movement matures, the organizations that support it are growing up, as well. Many projects, including Apache and Mozilla, have already created nonprofit organizations that support their communities. Other open source projects are also considering ways to establish nonprofits.[64]

Mozdev.org offers free project hosting and programming tools to developers to create Mozilla-based extensions that, licensed under an OSI licensing agreement, may or not be qualified for inclusion in upcoming releases of the Firefox browser and other applications. In short, Mozdev.org exists to feed Mozilla innovation. Mozdev.org has created space within Mozilla's framework, where programmers can develop and have ranked cross-platform applications. The distinction between Mozdev.org and Mozilla.org is simple: Mozilla.org is a site where, with regard to the Firefox browser, source code is developed, maintained, and improved; Mozdev.org supports programmers who, in the case of Firefox, create extensions with which the user can customize the browser to her or his needs. The more than 250 projects that are currently hosted at Mozdev.org are ranked based on the number of times each project is viewed.[65] Mozdev.org is similar to Mozilla.org in that it offers participants access to Version Control Systems and Bugzilla, the bug-tracking system. These resources, along with the requisite open-source licensing agreement, ensure that hosted projects are themselves infectious as open source projects. As does Mozilla.org, Mozdev.org also gives participants access to such communications tools as newsgroups, mailing lists, blogs, wikis, and other online forums. Mozdev.org also compiles statistics that describe the extent of a project's visibility and use in the Mozilla community.

An investigation into the benefits and challenges facing any organization that spawns either nonprofit or taxable subsidiaries in support of their missions is worthy of its own discrete study. The Mozilla Foundation created the Mozilla Corporation as a taxable subsidiary that, responsible for product development, marketing, and distribution of Mozilla products, dedicates its revenues to Mozilla.org.[66] A nonprofit organization, the National Geographic Society announced the founding of its own wholly owned, taxable subsidiary, National Geographic Entertainment, in 2007.[67] Our purpose in introducing Mozdev.org as an independent "innovation center" for Mozilla is simply to present the idea that, along with an individual's ambition to participate in the work of an organization like Mozilla, individuals also form and join consortiums that create further opportunities for participation on the part of individuals—whether we call individuals consumers, advocates, private citizens, constituents, and so on.

What Software Has to Teach Government

Introduction

Contemporary examples of crowdsourcing abound. Examples of mass participation in the public sector often take the form of wikis. Similar in its function to the Mozilla Knowledge Base, DailyStrength.org is a health network of individuals sharing symptoms and treatment advice. WikiHow.com reports at its site that over 50,000 articles have been written and edited primarily by self-selected volunteers in the ongoing compilation of the world's largest how-to manual. For-profit and nonprofit organizations seek ideas from the wisdom of groups. Originally a Web site designed to crowdsource ideas for Web-based businesses, Cambrian House claims to collaborate with its 50,000 online members not only to source entrepreneurial ideas, but also to develop the best of those ideas into businesses.

Knowledge As Power, DemocracyLab, and Govit are examples of Web sites designed to increase public participation in governmental decision making. The city of San Diego, California, is experimenting with participatory budget drafting by asking citizens to suggest money-saving measures.[68] Officials in federal agencies like the Transportation Security Administration (http://www.tsa.gov) are blogging with the public.

Mozilla is arguably the most successful open source project yet undertaken. Both in terms of the number of participants and the importance of the Firefox browser, Mozilla is worthy of attention. While Mozilla software is licensed to ensure its free redistribution and modification, what is unique about the Mozilla Project is that it is both *participatory* and *professional*. Ordinary people outside of the Mozilla organization collaborate in making and marketing the browser. The number of individuals who participate is far greater than ever before realized in any online project. But unlike many collaborative open source projects, Mozilla's distributed network of producers manages to turn out a product that millions of people rely on daily for their information. So for those who argue that ordinary people have neither the time nor the ability to participate in the hard work of governance, Mozilla may offer an instructive and timely counter-example, as well as a model for how to organize citizen participation in government.

We begin this section by identifying parallels between the technology used to create engagement for Firefox and the technological innovations used by the Obama administration to solicit public participation in a variety of programs. In applying the Mozilla model to government, we then identify some contemporary examples of participatory governance. Which government agencies already use crowdsourcing in their decision-making processes? What do they have in common with Mozilla from an organizational standpoint? Answers to these questions help us speculate as to which other agencies might benefit from open source strategies. Finally, we make recommendations on how to stimulate Mozilla-like public participation, and address scenarios in which the Mozilla model may not be appropriate and useful in the public and civic sectors.

A Philosophy of Experimentation

Despite the fact that open source has its roots in the advocacy of hackers in the 1960s, the practices that we associate with open source continue to be in currency (or are popular once again). This is owing in part to the fact that open source is by its nature not only a growing set of forkable and portable tools, but also a philosophy of experimentation that is becoming increasingly palatable in traditional organizations. This is illustrated by the volume of new projects and now-abandoned projects conceived by user groups under the Mozilla banner, and also in the number of inactive projects that reside like ghost towns in source code repositories hosted by such organizations as Sourceforge (at sourceforge.net).[69]

An aspect of open source that promotes experimentation is the low cost of crowdsourcing once the infrastructure for an open source process is set up: put simply, when it is too expensive to find people, let them find themselves.[70] Let them gather on the basis of shared interests. The hundreds of user groups hosted at spreadfirefox.com were started voluntarily by advocates of the Firefox browser at little expense to Mozilla. What inspires individuals to voluntarily organize groups for the benefit of Mozilla? As we have discussed, one reason is the relevance of the Firefox browser in people's everyday lives. Does governmental policymaking have the saliency with people that their Web browsers do? Because the importance of government in daily life is an abstraction relative to the utility of a Web browser in connecting people with the Internet, experimentation begins with crowd-forming questions, whether those crowds are large or small. *Any question of public policy is the basis of an experiment in crowdsourcing.*

In trying to imagine the possible applications of crowdsourcing as a tool for increasing public participation in government policymaking, one begins by asking what issues are of public interest, even when the public interested in a particular policy issue is small or specialized, relative to the general public at large. We mentioned the example of participatory budget drafting in San Diego. While there is not yet any data on the success of that project, a city's fiscal planning is relevant to the lives of many people. Imagine more targeted, industry-specific questions. For example: a senator wants to draft frost protection legislation to insure crops grown in the state he represents. The experiment is the question or battery of questions addressed to stakeholders in the relevant industry. Maybe the issue is tenure for professors at state universities. Under the banner of the Department of Health and Human Services, what questions might the U.S. Administration on Aging ask families about their caretaking needs for their elders? Government-founded consumer blogs could be set up to address such issues as toy safety, erosion and landslide monitoring, and traffic congestion on interstate freeways. As we will see later in this section, when we describe some contemporary examples of open government, crowdsourcing and its attendant process of self-selection work well when the question posed to a constituency is a narrow and carefully targeted one.

Another powerful crowdsourcing tool is the contest. Contests motivate individuals to experiment and innovate. Just as Mozilla Campus Reps promote Mozilla Lab's Design Challenge, and Mozilla sponsors marketing contests at ImpactMozilla.com, in 2008 the District of Columbia ran "Apps for Democracy," a contest that challenged technologists to create useful software applications from open data feeds in the district's Data Catalog, a public repository accessed via a Web site offering links to dozens of operational data sets about the city. For $50,000 in prize money, innovators from the general public devised 47 new tools in 30 days.[71]

President Obama launched his administration in the spirit of experimentation. In the transition between the presidential election and inauguration, the change.gov Web site hosted six online participation projects that invited people to either post questions or answers to other posted questions. Join the Discussion ran three times. Open for Questions took place twice, culminating with the creation of the online Citizen's Briefing Book. In each case, public participation was bookended by videotaped responses from senior political officials inviting and then responding to questions from private citizens. The fact that each of these pilots was an iteration of an idea is the definition of a work in progress—an experiment. The number of questions posted by private citizens ran over one hundred thousand, though the clarity of these questions varied wildly. While there was no way to trace the impact of any policy input offered by the citizenry, the attempt to create online public participation in the political process was a historic first for a presidential transition.

Mybarackobama.com

Understanding what Mozilla has to teach us about how to create more effective participation has become a more relevant and urgent exercise. On January 21, 2009, President Barack Obama issued a "Presidential Memorandum on Transparent and Open Government."[72] In it he writes: "Government should be participatory." Echoing what we know from Mozilla and other open source projects, he affirms, "knowledge is widely dispersed in society." The memorandum goes on to call for executive departments and agencies to "offer Americans increased opportunities to participate in policymaking and to provide their Government with the benefits of their collective expertise and information."

The "open government" ethic emerging in the first days of the Obama administration came as no surprise given the highly participatory nature of the U.S. presidential campaign and the transition from George W. Bush's presidency—an administration widely criticized for its lack of transparency—to the Obama administration. In the run up to the 2008 presidential election, Barack Obama made Web 2.0 capabilities—Web pages for online communication, Facebook and MySpace pages for social networking, and YouTube clips to air advertisements and presidential debates—an integral part of his campaign. He took full advantage of Web 2.0 tools and methods to connect supporters with one another and encourage people to build a movement for change.

When Senator Obama announced his candidacy on February 10, 2007, his campaign published mybarackobama.com. The Web site invited the public to submit policy suggestions and to blog about the campaign, as well as to upload pictures. The campaign also encouraged people to use Twitter, Facebook, and other technologies to make the campaign their own, rather than trying to control it from the center. An epigraph on the home page quoted then-Senator Barack Obama: "I'm asking you to believe not just in my ability to bring about real change in Washington . . . I'm asking you to believe in yours."[73] Some volunteers took it upon themselves to set up several campaign offices and ran ground operations without any assistance from the Obama campaign headquarters in Chicago.[74] This echoes the work of the Mozilla user groups, as well as the collaboration between Mozilla.org and Mozdev.org.

Mybarackobama.com had an important administrative component to it, one that is in widespread use on many Web sites: all visitors were asked to create accounts. This is one key step in identifying emergent (or "recursive") publics. A recent paper by Britt Blaser, David Weinberger, and Joe Trippi discusses the six stages in the transformation of campaign site visitors from Web surfer to political activist: (1) Readers, (2) Critics, (3) Creators, (4) Joiners, (5) Doers, and (6) Leaders.[75] *Readers* visiting campaign sites are casually and occasionally tracking the campaign. *Critics* scrutinize the site itself and may comment on articles. *Creators* are more active, entering into dialogs on interactive Weblogs. *Joiners, Doers,* and *Leaders* involve themselves in the campaign to the extent that their participation ceases to be exclusively online. They not only join groups in their physical communities, but also initiate projects designed to promote their chosen candidates and issues. Based on this theoretical hierarchy, visitors who created accounts at mybarackobama. com actually were more inclined toward active roles—creators, joiners, doers, and leaders—in the campaign. As registered members, they could locate meetings in their communities, blog at the Web site, and coordinate canvassing activities.

Mybarackobama.com also took advantage of listservs to convene over 5,400 experts and organize them into policy subcommittees to offer advice and write position papers for the campaign.[76] Because the Obama transition team solicited experts, this is not a strong example of self-selection. However, this is an instance of Mozilla-like architecture: participants formed their own committees, creating a hierarchy of small groups—each with its own hierarchy—that constellated the Obama agenda. Subcommittees focused on topics such as telecommunications, green energy, disabilities, and climate change. Like Mozilla, the listservs were not without central coordination. Each list, which equated to a subcommittee, had a moderator who, in turn, reported to a committee chair. But the committees themselves had lists to which any member could post announcements and news. In other words, the telecommunications subcommittee had a chair and a listserv, but that group also belonged to the much larger Telecommunications, Media, and Technology (TMT) committee and list. The subcommittees worked on more detailed drafting projects while the committee activity was more focused on the exchange of stories and get-out-the-vote activities.

The fact that these experts were recruited echoes the importance that Mozilla places on the ability of leaders to steer volunteer experts toward underrepresented projects. Furthermore, the assigning of leaders to teams that covered such a broad spectrum of topics reflects the essential nature of modularity in organizing an open source process. In effect, each area of inquiry—telecommunications, climate change, and so on—became its own innovation center, where each center may benefit from its own open source infrastructure. Mozilla is an aggregation of innovation centers.

From early February of 2007 until Election Day on November 4, 2008, the constituency base of the Obama campaign created approximately 2 million user profiles and 35,000 volunteer groups at mybarackobama.com. In the same period, volunteers organized some 200,000 off-line events via the Web site.[77] Though it is difficult to qualify the influence of time on rates of participation, it is worth noting that the presidential campaign, beginning in late 2006 and early 2007 when public figures began to formally announce their candidacies, lasted nearly two years. Given this timeframe and the centrality of public participation in the Obama campaign, the effort facilitated at mybarackobama.com resembles the earliest iterations of the Mozilla Project as an open source start-up.

The New Administration

There are many potential and real parallels between the online infrastructures and—with regard to how best to interface with their recursive publics—the stated missions of the Mozilla Project and the Obama administration. Both enterprises identify the Internet as a public resource essential to increasing communication with their constituencies, maximizing the transparency of the operations, and inspiring public participation in the development of their products and services.

When he took office, Barack Obama brought with him a "new media" team—originally an ad hoc group of technologists who had managed his Web presence throughout the presidential campaign. On January 20, 2009, this team assumed the management of whitehouse.gov.[78] Owned by the U.S. government and launched as the official Web site of the White House in 1994, whitehouse.gov is the purview of the presiding administration, which controls its content. Like the Mozilla Project's use of mozilla.org, the Obama White House is using its Web site as a primary tool for promoting transparency and public participation in its overall enterprise.

A month after President Obama's inauguration, Macon Phillips, the incoming director of new media at the White House, appeared in an online video posted at whitehouse.gov to promote the site as a public resource dedicated to opening the lines of communication between private citizens and the executive branch of government.[79] In addition to its traditional content—vignettes about American history, historical photographs, press briefings, executive orders, announcements of appointments and nominations, and the like—whitehouse.gov highlights pressing legislation before Congress and airs "Your Weekly Address," a video address by President Obama. Whitehouse.gov features the White House blog, a medium new to the Web site that affords visitors access to commentary by White House staff on a wide range of contemporary issues, including civil rights, national defense, the economy, education, the environment, foreign policy, immigration, and poverty. The Web site also provides links to the various social networking tools to which the White House officially subscribes, including Facebook, Twitter, Flickr, MySpace, YouTube, iTunes, and LinkedIn. The centralization of online access points to content via new media at whitehouse.gov echoes the Mozilla Project's use of mozilla.org as its online headquarters.

In a change closely linked with the mission of the president's new media team, on May 11, 2009, President Obama announced a new name for the Office of Public Liaison, a White House office established under President Nixon to manage public affairs between the executive branch and public interest groups. Under its new designation as the White House Office of Public Engagement, the office "will serve as the front door to the White House through which ordinary Americans can participate and inform the work of the President."[80] This change of name heralded a change of mission: the Obama administration is using the revised office to manage implementation of the Presidential Memorandum on Transparent and Open Government and to work with agencies on becoming more transparent to and collaborative with American taxpayers.

Like the Mozilla Project in its infancy, the Obama administration is a work in progress, one that is expediently redefining offices and personnel to increase government transparency through the use of the everyday technologies that enable private citizens to communicate with their elected representatives.

Even before President Obama took office, he made a public commitment to transparency in government. During the transition to the new administration, Senator Obama's new media team published the minutes of meetings held by the president-elect at change.gov. The Web site also hosted an interactive blog through which visitors could post opinions about public policy. Visitors were also invited to respond to the Citizens Briefing Book (CBB), a program that will be described in the next section of this report.

Before turning to the CBB, it is worth noting that the content of change.gov was licensed to the public at large via a Creative Commons Attribution 3.0 License.[81] Creative Commons (CC) is a nonprofit organization that, in its effort to increase the range of published works that others can legally use as resources in their own work, advocates open source practices in industries other than software development. Operating in a manner similar to the open source licenses described in this report, a CC license allows proprietors of published content to designate which of their proprietary rights they reserve, and which of those rights they waive for the benefit of projects unaffiliated with their own. After the Obama administration transferred much of the content of change.gov to whitehouse.gov, third-party content on whitehouse.gov was relicensed under a CC license.[82] In the same press release that announced the new name and the revised functions of the Office of Public Engagement, the Obama administration also announced the publication of the results of CBB, an early experiment in transparency conducted by the new administration.

President Obama and the Citizen's Briefing Book

An example of the use of crowdsourcing to gather public feedback on high-visibility, national issues (and to at least promote transparency and participation) comes from Barack Obama's transition to the Oval Office. The Citizen's Briefing Book (CBB) project ran at the change.gov Web site during the last week of the transition period. The CBB asked the public to submit policy suggestions in one or more of over two dozen categories, including civil rights, education, national defense, the environment, immigration, taxes, poverty, and veterans affairs. The design of the CBB Web site, which employed a commercially available product developed by Salesforce.com that companies like Starbucks use to solicit customer and employee feedback, enabled private citizens to submit suggestions and rank the proposals of others. Michael Strautmanis, director of public liaison and intergovernmental affairs for the transition, reported that over 70 million people participated.[83] At the end of the comment period, which lasted a week, the then-president-elect's transition team posted a video reply on YouTube to some of the more popular suggestions collected at the CBB Web site, including ideas about green jobs, high-speed rail, and energy efficiency.[84]

Narrated by Nancy Sutley, chair-designee for the White House Council on Environmental Quality, this response illustrates *one* aspect of the Mozilla model at work: private citizens were able to identify the national issues they deemed most relevant to their daily lives, or that most resonated with their worldviews. In addition to transportation and the environment, the most popular comments posted in the CBB centered on ending mari-

juana prohibition, the efficacy of government-sponsored absti-
nence education in sex education programs, taxes, the place of
insurance companies in healthcare reform, and whether or not
President Obama would advocate the prosecution of members
of the Bush administration for torture, illegal wiretapping, and
misleading the country into war.

Though this opportunity on the part of private citizens to
identify crucial issues did suggest a new administration dedicated to increased transparency in government, the CBB nevertheless was designed more as a national poll than a conduit
through which private citizens could participate in policymaking. In focusing exclusively on transportation and the environment in the YouTube response, the incoming administration
used the occasion of the CBB to spotlight issues that would be
prominently addressed in the economic stimulus package
passed in February 2009. Despite the inherent limitations of the
CBB to increase public participation in governmental decision
making, the incoming administration's strategic selection of
issues exemplifies such core open source principles as transparency, forking, and portability:

- Issues that were not emphasized in the incoming administration's video response were nevertheless published as they were
ranked.
- The CBB created public deliberation separate from President
Obama's immediate agenda.
- The CBB created a document that in the spirit of a source code
repository could be fashioned as a public registry, from which
ideas might be cribbed, reproduced, and distributed.

• Such a public registry could be appropriated, republished at a different location on the Web, discontinued in its original capacity, and launched as a new and separate registry.

Keeping these points in mind, it is helpful, if only as a thought experiment, to contrast the function of the CBB with characteristics of open source processes that make Mozilla successful, even if such a comparison is irrelevant to the intended use of the CBB. Relative to the Mozilla experience, the administration's question regarding which issues private citizens find most pressing is an open-ended one. To truly embrace the Mozilla model, the administration would need to assign issues to smaller, ad hoc groups—groups that act as discrete innovation centers, much like modules under Mozilla's module ownership system or profit centers comprised by a single corporation.

From the perspective of a governing body, crowdsourcing is a "pull" strategy—one that solicits feedback on a narrow topic, such as efficiency in patent review at the United States Patent and Trademark Office (USPTO) or watershed health, as monitored by the U.S. Environmental Protection Agency (EPA). When the call for feedback is monolithic, it dilutes the process of self-selection that identifies issue-specific experts in the crowd. Furthermore, it renders a private citizen's access to issue-specific leadership circuitous, if not improbable. The subject matter addressed by the federal government at large is modular by dint of its organization into agencies. Agencies are themselves modular. At EPA.gov, the EPA publishes advice and solicits feedback on how best to protect the environment in a variety of settings, including homes, schools, and the workplace. With regard to gardening, the EPA solicits feedback and recommends strategies for saving energy, reducing air pollution, conserving water, recycling materials, and safely using toxic pesticides.[85] To identify each of these topics as its own innovation center recalls characteristics of open-source software development that may be applicable to open government. Here we use the term *open source* more generally as a philosophy that, having been established an approach to software development, may be applied to the concept of open government:

- Open source integrates the distribution of products and/or services with the needs, lifestyles, and expertise of the public it serves.
- Open source operates in the public eye as a public resource.
- Open source as a process solicits the knowledge of individuals and groups with specific interests and expertise, making those individuals self-selecting because they can only volunteer their feedback on issues about which they are truly knowledgeable.
- Open source as a process depends on modularity—the dividing of tasks into manageable and thematically or technically specific projects.
- Open source requires an online structure—a set of protocols by which volunteer feedback is organized.
- Open source as a managerial structure is most effective as a top-down, hierarchical organization, one in which leadership steers participation and makes final decisions.

With regard to this final point and the centrality of self-selection in an open source approach to governance, it is important to recall that Mozilla does at times recruit experts from its community to work on specific projects. Self-selection is not in opposition to the solicitation of experts. Self-selection occurs within a pool of like-minded individuals, who make up a sub-community that is defined by a skill set.

The Open Government Initiative: Whitehouse.gov Revisited

As part of President Obama's Open Government Initiative, the new administration launched an online public consultation process designed to involve private citizens in the development of policies and practices that will increase transparency in governance, public participation in governmental decision making, and collaboration between inter- and intra-governmental agencies.[86] At whitehouse.gov, individuals were invited to participate in a three-phase process to aid the administration in the design and implementation of new protocols in open-government development.

The first phase, "Brainstorm," asked self-selected participants to submit recommendations on how to make government more open, and to rate the recommendations of their peers. The second phase, "Discuss," gave participants the opportunity to express their opinions on the many ideas captured in the first phase. The final phase, "Draft," enabled participants to collaborate via a wiki in the drafting of "recommendations that translate good ideas and lofty principles into specific actions that can be taken to achieve open government."[87] Specific topics included "Transparency Principles: Defining Transparency," "Citizen Participation in Government Decision Making: Creating New Opportunities to Engage," "Transparency Governance: Institutionalizing Transparency," "Strengthening Civic Participation: Training People to Participate," "Prizes: Creating Incentives for Public-Private Partnerships," "New Technologies and Participation: Enabling Participation with New Media," and "Online Public Participation in Agency Rulemaking/E-Rulemaking." Whitehouse.gov highlights important aspects of the Mozilla model, as we apply it to government:

- Volunteers are self-selected.
- The process for participation is clearly defined.
- Areas of inquiry were divided into categories (modules), maximizing the volunteers' ability to choose the subjects best suited to their experiences and skills, and thus to *specialize*.
- Volunteer recommendations are rated by the community; peer review is central to the process. Participants are given the ability to flag peer recommendations that seem off topic.
- Participants are given the ability to introduce new topics.
- The concept of forking was realized through a wiki that allowed participants to borrow sentences from peers and, with attribution, incorporate them into their own recommendations.
- Facilitators of the process published clear protocols—advice, recommendations—to volunteers on how to maximize the effectiveness of their contributions.
- Facilitators published an explanation of how feedback would be used by those who make final decisions.
- Final draft recommendations were reviewed by internal moderators, published for comment by the public, and circulated for interagency comment.

Some Contemporary Examples of Collaborative Governance

In considering Mozilla, a template begins to emerge that may in a few cases be identified as already at work in government. Faced with a crippling backlog of patent applications, the United States Patent and Trademark Office (USPTO) has in recent years instituted a pilot program known as Peer-to-Patent that, commensurate with Mozilla's crowdsourcing efforts, invites the public into the patent examination process.[88] Anyone can become a public reviewer by visiting the Peer-to-Patent Web site. Upon registering, public reviewers join teams akin to Mozilla's modules and contribute to the evaluation of inventions in their areas of knowledge. The expertise required to participate meaningfully in any one capacity creates a natural process of self-selection. Because public reviewers work in teams, they are responsible for vetting one another's contributions to the evaluation process. Individuals gain stature through the quality of their contributions, as determined via a formal rating system. Despite the established relevance of volunteer contributions, the final decisions on whether or not to grant a patent remains with the official patent examiner.[89] As with the Mozilla Project, the Peer-to-Patent pilot relies on technologists from around the country (and the world), who enthusiastically volunteer their expertise to the USPTO via the Internet. The entire program is online at peertopatent.org.

Similarly, the EPA crowdsources the expertise of private citizens by training them to monitor the quality of water in estuaries, lakes, streams, and wetlands in their local communities, and to report their findings to the appropriate public or private organizations.[90] The EPA educates potential volunteers about bioassessment by publishing fact sheets, monitoring methodologies, and resource guides at its Web site. Individuals join or start project groups in their communities by contacting project coordinators through the listserver known as "The Volmonitor."[91]

The examples of Peer-to-Patent and the EPA's volunteer water-monitoring program share several characteristics with the Mozilla model:

- The USPTO and EPA are tasked with solving complex problems that require interdisciplinary activities.
- At both the USPTO and the EPA, the use of volunteer experts requires a more granular (or modular) and focused set of practices, so that it is possible to clearly define and recruit for the roles available to private citizens.
- The USPTO and the EPA create group-based projects by connecting volunteers with each other.
- Despite the use of networks of private citizens, government agencies are still responsible for coordinating policymaking, and must remain central to the decision-making process, while taking advantage of volunteer feedback at the periphery.
- Both agencies solicit volunteers from a relatively unlimited and geographically dispersed pool of experts and enthusiasts.
- While the number of people who potentially can participate in any one project is large, the number of people who do participate in a single project is small.
- Volunteers choose what project they want to work on, and when they want to work on it.

A point of contrast between the EPA and both Mozilla and the USPTO concerns *locale*. Because the EPA's reach is national, it too benefits from federated participation. The work of volunteer water monitors takes place in the field. The EPA facilitates collaboration between small groups and regional organizations. As such, a geographically unlimited community may also be described from the point of view of a federal agency as a *network* of geographically *delimited* populations, a point that raises interesting questions about how the federal government might broker collaboration between private citizens and regional government agencies. How might federal agencies crowdsource expertise and assign that expertise to state and local programs? How might networks of delimited populations multiply opportunities for private citizens to participate in national service projects?

The example of volunteer bioassessment raises one more point of comparison between these organizations. Traditionally, aquatic biologists work alone or with an assistant. The assignment of groups of volunteers to bioassessment projects makes it possible for a federal or state agency to monitor many locations at once. Furthermore, volunteers tend to monitor waters where they live or vacation, so that they are regularly engaged in the task they have selected for themselves, and can in some cases monitor the health of a body of water over time.[92] This fact further captures an idea implicit in the motivations of volunteers involved with Mozilla and the USPTO: Programmers contribute code, technologists and hobbyists alike scrutinize patent applications, and environmentalists monitor watersheds because these activities construct their identities.

The Obama Network after the Election

In his blog posting on November 3, 2008, David Lazer, associate professor of public policy at Harvard's Kennedy School of Government, and director of the Program on Networked Governance, posed the question, "What happens to the Obama network after the election?"[93] On the eve of the election, Lazer estimated that there were an average of 4,000 *active* Obama supporters—what Joe Trippi would label *Leaders*—in each Congressional district in the United States. Other journalists and public intellectuals blogged about the use of the millions of people who volunteered to help the Obama campaign. The journalist Dan Froomkin called for a "Wiki White House":[94]

The goal should be to create a process whereby good ideas, relevant personal stories, informed opinions and perhaps even consensus on some issues can bubble up from the public. And while that may sound impossible, organizations like Wikipedia provide one model for handling vast quantities of user-submitted content with great if not perfect success. That model calls for a huge number of community volunteers working under the guidance of a small number of staffers. The White House is uniquely positioned to mobilize a small army of volunteers to monitor public comments should it choose that route.

A month after President Obama's inauguration, Blaser, Weinberger, and Trippi proposed a virtual network of the 435 U.S. Congressional districts.[95] Bringing the commentary of each of these critics to bear, the possibility of a Mozilla-like approach to participatory governance emerges.

In discussing the community of users dedicated to the Firefox browser, we saw that volunteer developers were variously active or, rather, that they became active when they identified problems that they felt qualified to work on. Despite the occasional nature of their participation, the fact that they would volunteer from time to time in the future meant the perpetuation of the project that defines their community. The classification of citizens according to which tier they occupy in the progression to political activist supports the notion that individuals choose when and how they will participate. Those who are most active—the Leaders at the top of the ladder, or the estimated 4,000 active Obama supporters in each of the 435 Congressional districts—are comparable to the most active programmers in the Mozilla development community; they are the module owners, peers, and committers. Imagine uniting their electoral counterparts under Froomkin's "Wiki White House."

Earlier in this report, in discussing the EPA's effort to involve private citizens in the monitoring of watersheds in their local communities, we introduced the idea of federated participation, by which a federal agency may describe a geographically unlimited community as a network of geographically delimited populations. The EPA brokers collaboration between private citizens (working in small groups) and regional agencies. A virtual network of Congressional districts could begin with the federal, online coordination of volunteers in their districts.

Potential Limitations of Crowdsourcing

It is tempting to say that the potential of crowdsourcing is unlimited. Maybe the greatest challenge of this discussion is the identification of those instances where open source strategies such as crowdsourcing *definitively* cannot instruct government.

This is true for at least two reasons: the proliferation of successful and/or novel crowdsourcing projects in both the public and
private sectors and the fact that open source projects character-
istically are experimental.

Any theory of open government raises questions about repre-
sentation and inclusiveness. One could argue that a ranking
system used by participants to vote community contributions
up or down could be exploited to give undue influence to a few
well-organized participants. Rating and ranking systems of citizen input may in some cases deny individuals the right to participate. Group-based participation systems, while potentially
more manageable and useful, could also impede the individual
First Amendment right to participate. For example, an individual who wishes to submit a piece of prior art to the Peer-to-Patent pilot, and has that submission rated down by the crowd,
may feel that she has been denied her right to participate in the
evaluation of a patent application. Of course, the integrity of
such a complaint would depend on when the participation process was understood to have started: participation may be the
right to introduce a proposal and have that proposal reviewed
by peers. Continued participation may be contingent on the
outcome of such peer review.

Another limitation is conceivable. Advocates and enthusiasts
working in relatively esoteric areas of national interest might
find that their issues are always ranked below headline-grabbing
topics. On January 13, 2009, an individual who was monitoring
the CBB during the comment period posted the following message on the blog at nasawatch.com:

Right now there are a few [posts] regarding NASA and space exploration but not enough votes to rise to the top. I just wanted to let you know about this with hopes that you would make a post about it. Your website reaches a large pro-space audience and maybe with that kind of exposure the space exploration ideas will have a chance to reach our President-elect.[96]

This citizen's concerns are real and reasonable. At the same time, the CBB inspired her or him to take action and draw attention to the issue of space in another forum. This blog posting supports the open source idea that effective public deliberation is not relegated by a controlling interest, but can spread virally to many forums, potentially inspiring new issue-centric advocacy groups.

Another possible side effect of increased public participation in governmental decision making is the potential rise in lawsuits known as *SLAPPs* (Strategic Lawsuits Against Public Participation). A SLAPP is usually a civil complaint or a counterclaim filed against someone who is critical of the plaintiff's enterprise. Though such lawsuits rarely are legally successful, they can be effective in silencing critics by encumbering them with legal expenses. For instance, a real estate developer might claim that a petition signatory aligned against his project was interfering with his contract. When such SLAPPs are brought against individuals who have participated in government crowdsourcing projects, it is known as *crowdslapping*.[97]

One final unknown with regard to crowdsourcing has to do with the unintended consequences of mobilizing a crowd. In 2008, the state of Texas set up a network of Internet cameras so that the general public could monitor the border with Mexico for illegal aliens and report suspicious activity to local authorities. This is a clear example of crowdsourcing.[98] The use of the Internet in mobilizing people against people may have unforeseen consequences, such as vigilantism.

Transparency: Toward Open Source Governance

The creation of an online forum, and ultimately the formation of a recursive public, begins with an organization's open call to a large, undefined group. An emergent, self-organizing public need not be defined by geography or proximity, but it will always coalesce around shared interests. In the abstract, the Mozilla model of participatory governance requires that government crowdsources expertise in the creation of passionate, self-organizing groups that represent the interests of larger constituencies. Government inspires private citizens to participate by creating a system that connects a small group with a government agency that, with the aid public feedback, is working to solve a specific problem.

The rise of participatory governance is predicated on the political concept of transparency. Openness equals transparency. The work of government must be made public if participation is to ensue. In concluding our discussion of Mozilla and the applicability of its open source practices to government, we ask the following question: Who makes transparency happen? We end with this question because transparency as a responsibility shared by the public and private sectors is the basis—the genesis—of public participation in governmental decision making.

In a panel discussion on January 9, 2009, at the Google headquarters in Washington, DC, Ellen Miller, executive director of the Sunlight Foundation, stated, "Transparency is government's responsibility."[99] A partial timeline of the legislative history of public transparency in the United States—beginning with the formation of the Government Accountability Office in 1921, and continuing with Administrative Procedure Act of 1946, the passage of the Freedom of Information Act in 1966 (and its subsequent amendments in 1996, 2002, and 2007), the Government Performance Results Act of 1993, the Government in the Sunshine Act of 1994, and the Federal Funding Accountability and Transparency Act of 2006—helps to narrate the history of Congress working to fulfill its responsibility of transparency. Laws such as the Clinger-Cohen Act (The Information Technology Management Reform Act of 1996), the 2001 Information Quality Act, and the e-Government Act of 2002 place public accessibility to information in the context of technology in the Internet Age. Beyond legislation, regulations that are open for public comment and final rules are available at the regulations.gov Web site. Today, President Obama's agenda is published at whitehouse.gov.

In a book called *Full Disclosure: The Perils and Promise of Transparency*, authors Archon Fung, Mary Graham, and David Weil describe another government strategy to increase public awareness of a variety of issues, including corporate and campaign finance, product safety, toxicity levels in drinking water, school performance, and terrorism-threat levels. "Targeted transparency" is the publication by the government of factual information about the social, commercial, and political interests that most affect the lives of private citizens.[100] Writing about *Full Disclosure* for *The American Prospect*, Professor Paul Starr situated this concept in another loose timeline in the history of public transparency:

The first-generation transparency policies of the 1960s and '70s—right-to-know laws, such as the Freedom of Information Act—gave the public access to previously restricted data and documents. Targeted transparency policies enacted in the '80s and after went a step further by requiring business and government to disclose standardized forms of information relevant to organizational performance. More recently, a third generation of efforts has emerged that the authors call "technology-enabled collaborative transparency." Instead of passively receiving information, consumers and the public can now actively create it by pooling their own data and experience. And in contrast to the relatively inflexible and slow systems created under targeted transparency laws, the new approach uses computers and the Internet to provide real-time information that individuals can customize for their own use.[101]

Culminating with the rise of "technology-enabled collaborative transparency," this chronology approaches but does not encapsulate the extent to which collaborative transparency has required collaboration between government and private citizens. There are two reasons why. First, the collaboration entailed in technology-enabled collaborative transparency is neither top-down nor bottom-up—the terms hardly apply—as it is not in service of any particular organization or agency. The collaborators are the crowd. The roles they may play are not defined and aggregated in a process developed to realize the goals of a larger organization. In contrast, Mozilla, like a government, is the centralizing authority of its enterprise. Mozilla offers individuals a variety of ways to participate. It puts people into collaboration with each other in the maintenance of its public's assets.

To understand the second reason that Mozilla represents a somewhat different strain of transparency as an approach to engendering participation, we return to Ellen Miller's position that transparency is the responsibility of government. Whether or not this is true, an accurate history of public participation in the United States depends on the contributions of organizations from outside of government that we may call *participation brokers*—organizations that act as intermediaries between government and its constituencies.

With regard to the specific issue of transparency, there are many examples of such brokers. Dedicated to voter services, citizen education, and "an open governmental system that is representative, accountable and responsive," the League of Women Voters was founded by Carrie Chapman Catt in 1920, months before the passage of the Nineteenth Amendment.[102] Serving as the Washington, DC bureau chief for a cable industry trade journal, Brian Lamb founded C-SPAN in 1979.[103] C-SPAN put Congress on TV. In 2006, Ellen Miller and attorney Michael Klein founded The Sunlight Foundation as a 501(c)(3) educational organization. The foundation hosts an interactive blog, links to open source coders dedicated to software projects that increase the transparency of government, and links to online databases that publish government data in useable formats.[104] In 2008, with the aid of a grant from the Sunlight Foundation, Sarah Schacht founded Knowledge As Power (KAP), an organization that, among other things, tracks legislation in the state of Washington.[105]

Each of these organizations aims to increase civic engagement through citizen education. Their collective purpose is so obvious and so aligned with government's supposed responsibility of transparency that one would think they were the innovations of government. One can imagine—maybe somewhat idealistically—the U.S. House of Representatives coming up with the idea of turning on the TV cameras. Equally idealistic but not utopic, one can imagine the federal government setting up KAP-like agencies in every state. (The work of NGOs such as Knowledge As Power further suggests the potential of the federal government to broker collaboration between private citizens and regional government agencies. The most active volunteers in each district could coordinate the publication of federal legislation on a state-by-state basis, an idea that approximates the independent but coordinated efforts of user groups in the Mozilla model.)

Though not exclusively an example of transparency, Peer-to-Patent is unique as an example of participation brokering because the broker, New York Law School, is an NGO that by way of peertopatent.org enlists private citizens (to form small, task-oriented groups) to participate in the work of government. Peer-to-Patent has proven to be such a worthy experiment that one wonders if the USPTO will ever cut out the middleman, and bring the program in-house. If it did, it would be internalizing a structure of hierarchical management that relies on collaborative, volunteer participation. The point here is not (yet) that the USPTO *should* take over the reins of the Peer-to-Patent pilot, or that Congress should necessarily found regional, KAP-like agencies. The point is that the responsibility of transparency is *shared*.

We see this shared sense of responsibility in the relationship between Mozilla.org and Mozdev.org, through which the Mozdev Community Organization brokers participation between volunteer programmers and Mozilla.org by hosting projects. New York Law School mirrors this relationship by (again) soliciting the expertise of volunteers in the examination of patent applications.

In Conclusion: Mozilla for Government

I

Mozilla organizes large-scale participation in the development of its software. The scope of participation is not captured by the total number of people working on Mozilla's overall mission, but rather, in the aggregation of a large number of small groups dedicated to many projects under the Mozilla banner. Development of the Firefox browser is organized under a module ownership system. Each module is governed by a system of hierarchical meritocracy. Each group houses its own hierarchy. Like profit centers in traditional corporations, each group or module operates as its own innovation center.

It follows that a large-scale poll like the one conducted under the auspices of the Citizens Briefing Book would be useful in identifying the issues to which private citizens pay the most attention. That said, an open source infrastructure is most effective when designed to manage public input on module- or agency-specific topics. Environmentally sound gardening techniques are not the purview of the White House, whereas the EPA is dedicated to increasing public awareness of green practices in the home and in public places. We see the abstract nature of the CBB in the scores of specific issues—from aerospace to the patent system—that were not represented.

Once a government agency like the EPA or the USPTO sets up an online infrastructure for public participation, it can work conscientiously with individuals in communities that are defined by skill sets. The door will also open to collaboration with industry-specific organizations. The assigning of tasks to self-organizing groups helps Mozilla improve its product, build market share, and educate the general public about its core mission. As articulated in the Mozilla Manifesto, that mission is as altruistic as it is commercial. The Mozilla community promotes a product and an experience, which perpetuates a sense of cohesion in a geographically dispersed population that is united by a shared sense of mission.

II

Open source participants are identified on the basis of their roles in a system of distributed peer review. From the top down, that hierarchy (in the Mozilla model) includes the module owner, the module owner's immediate peers, committers, and FLOSS developers from outside and within Mozilla proper. With the rare exception of individuals who are both employed by Mozilla and active in the development of a module, each of these roles is voluntary. The success of the module ownership system depends on the following concepts:

- People must know they have the option to participate.
- Participants choose their tasks. Based on their expertise and enthusiasm, they choose what they want to do, when they want to do it.

- Individuals are self-selected into self-organizing groups.
- Not everyone is involved all the time.
- The ratio of active participants to the total population of a community may be small.
- Participants may discover new roles as they acclimate to the community.
- Final decisions are made leaders—module owners, elected officials, editors, etc.

Each of these points is applicable to government. We see such organization in the examples of the USTPO and the EPA. Not everyone is paying attention to the health and wellbeing of watersheds. But there are those who are, just as there are those who have an interest in the innovations in their industries under review by the USTPO. Where participation is mutually beneficial to the organization, the volunteer, and the volunteer's community, there is a greater likelihood of engagement. The benefits of collaboration to Mozilla are clear: the input of proportionately small, self-selected groups makes public participation manageable.

The motivations of the volunteer are manifest in a variety of dichotomies: personal/professional, individual/civic, psychological/sociological. Participants are motivated by personal enrichment and a sense of community. That the Mozilla experience engenders civic-mindedness and, at the same time, opportunities for individuals to improve the technology they use in their everyday lives makes the Mozilla Project applicable to our understanding of the stated and implied goals of governmental agencies. Though government is not expressly in the business of product development and marketing, it does manage enterprises and offer services that are relevant to the everyday lives of citizens and may be improved through the feedback of constituencies that are meant to benefit from these services. Furthermore, government seeks to develop new programs based on the needs of the governed.

III

If government is to successfully proliferate its current services and innovate new policies, it may do so by collaborating with private citizens. While in the abstract the Internet enables geographically distributed communities to cohere around a common cause or interest, infrastructure is necessary for people working across a distance to become a community. With regard to this assertion, the Mozilla model makes the following points:

- Having a well-designed system by which individuals can contribute to the shared work of the group is essential to forging a recursive public.
- Such a system must be able to evolve.
- Without the ability to manage volunteer contributions online, an organization can ill afford to support public participation.
- Networked governance is organized with Web pages.
- Networked governance through Web pages provides group-based structures for collaboration on the Internet.

The Mozilla CVS provides the necessary technological architecture to support the community in its distributed work. Mozilla. org not only is the home of the source code repository, but also is a portal to other technical and nontechnical segments of the overall project, many of which operate as discrete Web sites.

Through these Web sites, Mozilla extends the open source idea beyond programming. Firefox's user community helps with marketing campaigns at spreadfirefox.com. The Mozilla Knowledge Base, a community-maintained (wiki) user manual, is online at support.mozilla.com.

IV

The collaboration between Mozilla and networked publics is governed through the licensing of intellectual property. An open source license creates recursion by guaranteeing the individual the use of licensed resources in his own innovations, in return for access to those innovations. Though the relevance of licensing to governance is subtle, an open source license does reflect two concepts crucial to the concept of innovation as a collaborative exercise: forking, by which a new project is created on the basis of an existing project, with or without the foreknowledge of the licensor; and portability, which ensures that an effective tool can be used "as is" for applications other than the one for which it was originally designed. The significance of these practices cannot be overstated in our understanding of Mozilla's success, as they allow an individual to choose the work she wants to do, when she wants do it, without her needing to be commissioned or sanctioned by Mozilla. This fact makes possible more aspects of the Mozilla model of governance:

- Open source licensing formalizes the relationship between an organization and its constituency.
- Open source licensing formalizes decentralized participation and what in many instances we may think of as *blind* collabora-

tion. (Mozilla need not know that a developer is working to improve the Firefox browser until that improvement is submitted for review.)[106]

• Because licensing makes possible decentralized participation, it helps to create a culture in which experimentation is rewarded and failure is tolerated.

This final point merits elaboration, as its ramifications for government are profound. Under a system of hierarchical meritocracy, voluntary contributions are induced and, when cogent, rewarded. The volunteer—the citizen or the "netizen"—incurs opportunity costs—experiments, succeeds, fails—and advances in the cybercommunity based on the usefulness of his contributions. His independence offsets the risks of innovation faced by the organization with which he means to collaborate. He experiments prior to peer review. Whether or not the original organization implements his innovation, he is free to use it himself, and to distribute it. Likewise:

• Participatory governance connects an organization with its constituency.

• Participatory governance inspires innovation beyond its own agenda, in part by putting constituents into contact with other constituents, without the chaperoning of the government agency.

V

An understanding of the term *netizen* begins to articulate what is quietly revolutionary about this system. A netizen is someone who is actively involved in online communities.[107] He or she is actively concerned with the health of the Internet: Is it free? Is it open? Is it available to everyone? How do we measure? He or she uses such online tools and forums as blogs, chat rooms, file sharing, and wikis to join virtual networks. Because of the centrality of technology in their everyday lives, netizens are very familiar with the use of these same technologies by political candidates and their campaigns. To use these communications technologies to follow and to some degree contribute to a campaign, a cause, or an idea in these times of cybercampaigning and virtual networks is to be self-politicizing.

The problem that arises is an old one, known by the term *digital divide*. Netizens, generally speaking, have the skills and resources to participate in online governance. In defining the digital divide, identifying these skills and resources as a way of differentiating netizens from individuals who cannot easily participate in online communities is difficult. Most basically, the term is used to compare netizens to individuals who do not have access to a computer and/or the Internet. Here, the digital divide may also suggest a gap between those who have access to broadband and those who do not. Defining the problem becomes increasingly complex when barriers to Internet access are associated with societal problems like poverty. The question is an obvious one: how does a system of collaborative governance that is dependent on its participants' use of technology include those individuals who are disenfranchised because they lack that technology?

Though an investigation of all of the factors that may contribute to a comprehensive understanding of the digital divide is beyond the scope of this report, it is relevant to return to some of the original motivations of early, open source activists. As described at the beginning of this report, the FSF—the organization inspired by Richard Stallman's GNU Project—contextualizes free software as the freedoms "to study how the program works, and adapt it to your needs"; "to redistribute [software] so you can help your neighbor"; and "to improve the program, and release your improvements (and modified versions in general) to the public, so that the whole community benefits."[108] As the FSF definition of free software goes on to state, "access to the source code is a precondition for this," just as access to the Internet is a precondition to the Mozilla Project's powerful conviction that "individuals must have the ability to shape their own experiences on the Internet"[109]—a tenet that has led individuals to translate online text into their native languages and individuals with disabilities to make meaningful suggestions as to how best the Mozilla Project may accommodate them in their use of the Firefox Web browser. Though these values cannot thoroughly address challenges posed by the digital divide, they do promote an ethos of participation that extends the open source concept beyond software to collaborative governance.

In sum, government is meant to enable everyone to participate equally. The Mozilla model of governance allocates responsibility based on an individual's contribution. A contributor is empowered through his ability to exploit the opportunity to participate. This calls into question our most fundamental assumptions about equality. In the Mozilla model, the administration of pure equality, where each contribution is given equal weight, is inconceivable. Nonhierarchical collaboration is inconsistent with productivity. The assignment of tasks based on comparative advantage among individuals—and reputation derived from merit—makes mass participation manageable. Mozilla's contribution to our understanding of democracy stems from the fact that the work it invites volunteers to undertake is various. Not everyone can do everything effectively. But the extension of community-based approaches to problem solving to more areas makes participatory governance increasingly interdisciplinary and, as such, promotes inclusivity.

VI

Though we demand of our government that it be transparent and accountable, a history of political and civic life in the United States reminds us that transparency sometimes requires an NGO-brokered relationship between private citizens and government. Netizens are predisposed to collaboration with the online organizations that strive to connect people and government. They are well positioned to receive government services via the media of Web sites and social networking tools. For an increasing number of people open source spreads collaboration beyond its own agenda (forking and portability), suggesting the potential for open government to create opportunities for civic engagement in direct alignment with—and beyond—its own agenda. It is for this reason that we may ask not only what software has to teach government, but also what open source has to teach private citizens who, through participation, want to foster greater transparency and accountability on the part of government. Every opportunity that Mozilla offers individuals to collaborate on a project is only as good as the willingness of those individuals, even if only a few at a time, to accept that offer and contribute both their time and knowledge as they see fit.

Notes

1. Justin Mann, "Firefox User Base Swells to 270 Million," *Techspot: PC Technology News and Analysis*, May 6, 2009, http://www.techspot.com/news/34599-firefox-user-base-swells-to-270-million.html (accessed September 30, 2009).

2. "Net Applications Market Share," http://marketshare.hitslink.com/report.aspx?qprid=1 (accessed January 3, 2009).

3. Al Fasoldt, "Netscape Makes Its Browser Free Again," *Technofile*, February 1998, http://aroundcny.com/technofile/texts/bit020198.html (accessed September 30, 2009).

4. "The GNU Manifesto," GNU Operating System, http://www.gnu.org/gnu/manifesto.html (accessed January 2, 2009).

5. "The Free Software Definition," GNU Operating System, http://www.gnu.org/philosophy/free-sw.html (accessed January 2, 2009).

6. Ian A. Murdock, "NNTP Subject: New Release under Development; Suggestions Requested," August 16, 1993, http://groups.google.com/group/comp.os.linux.development/msg/a32d4e2ef3bcdcc6 (accessed May 31, 2009).

7. Joe Klemmer, "A Short History of Linux Distributions," *LWN.net*, June 30, 2004, http://lwn.net/Articles/91371 (accessed September 30,

2009). Also see Adam J. Richter, "ANNOUNCE: Alpha Release of Turn-key Linux/GNU/X System on CDROM," *Kernel Trap*, November 24, 1992, http://kerneltrap.org/mailarchive/linux-activists/1992/11/25/1664 (accessed September 30, 2009).

8. Open Source Initiative, "The Open Source Definition," http://www.opensource.org/docs/osd (accessed December 20, 2008).

9. Open Source Initiative, "History of the OSI," http://www.opensource.org/history (accessed December 20, 2008).

10. Mozilla Project, "The Mozilla Manifesto," http://www.mozilla.org/about/manifesto (accessed November 5, 2008).

11. Janet Kornblum, "Netscape Sets Source Code Free," *CNET News*, March 31, 1998.

12. Christopher M. Kelty, *Two Bits: The Cultural Significance of Free Software* (Durham, NC: Duke University Press, 2008).

13. Ibid.

14. CVS is one of about five different systems that allow a large number of programmers to collaborate on a single project. CVS is a specific product classified under the broader rubric of Version Control System. CVS was the first system of its kind.

15. Mitchell Baker, personal interview, November 20, 2008.

16. Darryl K. Taft, "Startup Helps Assess Open-Source Projects," *eWeek*, July 13, 2006, http://www.week.com (accessed December 5, 2008).

17. Ohloh.net lists 152 front-end programmers. Eight hundred and twenty-four programmers work on "Mozilla Core" projects—the back end of the browser. Eighty-eight programmers work in the Mozilla Chrome category. SpiderMonkey is a key component of Firefox, and that lists 195 people involved. Firefox built for Mobile devices is code-named "Fennec." Firefox's built-in Web-page debugger is called "Firebug" and its 12 contributors are listed at Ohloh.net. Firefox also ships a "platform" library called XulRunner.

18. Steven Weber, *The Success of Open Source* (Cambridge, MA: Harvard University Press, 2004).

19. Frederick P. Brooks, *The Mythical Man-Month* (Boston: Addison-Wesley, 1975).

20. Eric S. Raymond, *The Cathedral and the Bazaar: Musings on Linux and Open Source by an Accidental Revolutionary* (Sebastopol, CA: O'Reilly and Associates, Inc., 1999).

21. Steven Weber, see note 18.

22. Eric S. Raymond, see note 20.

23. Asa Dotzler, personal interview, April 17, 2009.

24. Paul A. David and Joseph S. Shapiro, "Community-based Production of Open Source Software: What Do We Know about the Developers Who Participate?" October 17, 2008, http://ssrn.com/abstract=1286273.

25. Ibid.

26. Mozilla Project, see note 10.

27. Jon Brodkin, "Firefox Add-on Enhances Web for Visually Impaired," *Network World*, September 9, 2008, www.networkworld.com/news/2008/090908-firefox-visual-add.html. Also see "Accessibility Features of Firefox," *mozillaZine*, http://kb.mozillazine.org/Accessibility_features_of_Firefox (accessed April 2, 2009).

28. Asa Dotzler, see note 23.

29. Jens Rasmussen, Berndt Brehmer, and Jacques Leplat (eds.), *Distributed Decision Making: Cognitive Models for Cooperative Work* (New York: Wiley, 1991).

30. Mozilla Project, "Distributed Decision-Making: Mozilla Modules and Module Ownership," http://www.mozilla.org/hacking/module-ownership (accessed October 28, 2009).

31. Mitchell Baker, see note 15.

32. Ibid.

33. Asa Dotzler, see note 23.

34. Brian Behlendorf, personal correspondence, January 8, 2009.

35. Mozilla Project, "Becoming a Mozilla Committer," http://www .mozilla.org/hacking/committer/ (accessed October 30, 2009).

36. Ibid.

37. Asa Dotzler, see note 23.

38. Mozilla Project, "Mozilla.org Drivers," http://www.mozilla.org/ about/drivers (accessed January 8, 2009).

39. Mozilla Project, "Module Owners Activities Modules," https://wiki .mozilla.org/Module_Owners_Activities_Modules (accessed January 14, 2008).

40. There are also examples of proprietary forks. Working under an AT&T Unix source license, U.C. Berkeley's Computing Systems Research Group (CSRG) created Berkeley Software Distribution (BSD), a Unix operating system that was itself forked into many BSD variants, including OpenBSD, BSD OS, and MachTen. Unix-based NeXTStep became the MacIntosh OS 10 operating system by way of a BSD fork. BSD also spawned Solaris. Applications born from other projects include open-source content management systems, office suites, text editors, open-source instant messaging applications, and many other systems and protocols. See http://linuxmafia.com/faq/Licensing_and_Law/forking .html (accessed October 30, 2009).

41. Bugzilla.org, "Installation List," http://www.bugzilla.org/installation -list/ (accessed January 20, 2009).

42. David Tenser, "The Vision for SUMO, Part 2: Understanding the Bigger Picture," *SUMO Blog: The Support.Mozilla.com (SUMO) Project Blog*, http://blog.mozilla.com/sumo/2008/09/02/the-vision-for-sumo-2/ (accessed January 2, 2009).

43. Mozilla Project, "Mozilla Community," http://www.mozilla.org/community/ (accessed December 5, 2008).

44. David Tenser, see note 42.

45. Support.Mozilla.com, "How to Contribute," https://support.mozilla.com/en-US/kb/Approving+articles+and+edits (accessed on January 15, 2009).

46. David Tenser, see note 42.

47. Mozilla Project, see note 10.

48. "Spread Firefox | The Home of Firefox Community Marketing," http:///www.spreadfirefox.com/ (accessed January 3, 2009).

49. Compete, Inc., "Site Profile for Foxiewire.com," http://siteanalytics.compete.com/foxiewire.com/ (accessed January 15, 2009).

50. "For the Record," Spread Firefox | The Home of Firefox Community Marketing, http://www.spreadfirefox.com/fortherecord (accessed January 14, 2009).

51. Daniel Mintz, "Government 2.0: Fact or Fiction?" *The Public Manager* (Spring 2008).

52. "Interacting with One of the Web's Most Popular Pages," *Blog of Metrics*, http://blog.mozilla.com/metrics/ (accessed January 14, 2009).

53. "Campus Reps," Spread Firefox | The Home of Firefox Community Marketing, http://www.spreadfirefox.com/ (accessed January 3, 2009).

54. Jay Patel, "Watch Our Campus Reps Hit the Streets," *Jay's Blog*, http://blog.mozilla.com/jay/2008/12/26/watch-our-campus-reps-hit-the-streets/ (accessed January 11, 2009).

55. "Introducing the Design Challenge," *FoxieWire: Your Source for Daily Mozilla News*, http://www.foxiewire.com/Mozilla/Introducing_the_Design_Challenge (accessed January 11, 2009).

56. "Impact Mozilla Challenge," http://impactmozilla.com/ (accessed January 11, 2009).

57. "Welcome to a World without Oil," streaming video, http://world withoutoil.org/ (accessed January 12, 2009).

58. Andrew Chadwick, *Internet Politics: States, Citizens, and New Communication Technologies* (New York: Oxford University Press, 2006).

59. "Download Day 2008," Spread Firefox | The Home of Firefox Community Marketing, www.spreadfirefox.com/en-US/worldrecord (accessed January 12, 2009).

60. Jennifer Leggio, "Firefox 3 and Community: How Mozilla Used Social Networking to Set a World Record," *ZDNet*, July 8 2008, http://blogs.zdnet.com/feeds/?p=140 (accessed January 13, 2009).

61. "Internet Users Worldwide by Region, 2007–2012," *eMarketer* (January 2008) http://www.emarketer.com/ (accessed November 28, 2008).

62. "Fans of Mozilla Firefox," Facebook, http://www.facebook.com/pages/Mozilla-Firefox/14696440021 (accessed February 1, 2009).

63. David Boswell, Brian King, Ian Oeschger, Pete Collins, and Eric Murphy, *Creating Applications with Mozilla* (Sebastopol, CA: O'Reilly and Associates, Inc., 2002).

64. David Boswell, "How to Build a Nonprofit for Your Company," Policy DevCenter, http://oreillynet.com/policy/ (accessed April 15, 2009).

65. See http://www.mozdev.org/projects/top50.html (accessed October 30, 2009).

66. Frank Hecker, "The Mozilla Foundation Reorganization," http://hecker.org/mozilla/dot-reorg (accessed April 16, 2009).

67. "National Geographic Creates Entertainment Unit," http://press.nationalgeographic.com/pressroom/ (accessed April 16, 2009).

68. "A Message from Mayor Jerry Sanders," Sandiego.gov, http://www
.sandiego.gov/mayor/budgetsuggestions.shtml (accessed January 24,
2009).

69. Dawid Weiss, "Quantitative Analysis of Open Source Projects at
Source Forge," Poznan University of Technology, Poznan, Poland, 2005.

70. Though it is beyond the scope of this report, it is important to note
that start-up costs for an open source project can be considerable. Lotus
1–2–3 designer, cofounder of the Electronic Frontier Foundation, and
former Mozilla board member Mitch Kapor funded the development of
an open source PIM (personal information management) suite known as
Chandler for six years before abandoning the project. See Matt Asay,
"Mitch Kapor Bails on the Chandler Project," *CNET News*, January 9,
2009, http://news.cnet.com/8301-13505_3-9847739-16.html (accessed
September 23, 2009).

71. Peter Corbett, "Apps for Democracy Yields 4,000% ROI in 30 Days
for D.C. Gov," iStrategyLabs, November 15, 2009, http://www.istrate
gylabs.com/2008/11/apps-for-democracy-yields-4000-roi-in-30-days-for-
dcgov/ (accessed October 28, 2009).

72. Presidential Memorandum on Transparent and Open Government,
January 21, 2009, http://www.whitehouse.gov/the_press_office/Trans
parencyandOpenGovernment (accessed September 23, 2009):

THE WHITE HOUSE
Office of the Press Secretary
For Immediate Release January 21, 2009
January 21, 2009
MEMORANDUM FOR THE HEADS OF EXECUTIVE DEPARTMENTS AND
AGENCIES
SUBJECT: Transparency and Open Government
My Administration is committed to creating an unprecedented level of openness
in Government. We will work together to ensure the public trust and establish
a system of transparency, public participation, and collaboration. Openness will
strengthen our democracy and promote efficiency and effectiveness in Govern-
ment.

Government should be transparent. Transparency promotes accountability and provides information for citizens about what their Government is doing. Information maintained by the Federal Government is a national asset. My Administration will take appropriate action, consistent with law and policy, to disclose information rapidly in forms that the public can readily find and use. Executive departments and agencies should harness new technologies to put information about their operations and decisions online and readily available to the public. Executive departments and agencies should also solicit public feedback to identify information of greatest use to the public.

Government should be participatory. Public engagement enhances the Government's effectiveness and improves the quality of its decisions. Knowledge is widely dispersed in society, and public officials benefit from having access to that dispersed knowledge. Executive departments and agencies should offer Americans increased opportunities to participate in policymaking and to provide their Government with the benefits of their collective expertise and information. Executive departments and agencies should also solicit public input on how we can increase and improve opportunities for public participation in Government.

Government should be collaborative. Collaboration actively engages Americans in the work of their Government. Executive departments and agencies should use innovative tools, methods, and systems to cooperate among themselves, across all levels of Government, and with nonprofit organizations, businesses, and individuals in the private sector. Executive departments and agencies should solicit public feedback to assess and improve their level of collaboration and to identify new opportunities for cooperation.

I direct the Chief Technology Officer, in coordination with the Director of the Office of Management and Budget (OMB) and the Administrator of General Services, to coordinate the development by appropriate executive departments and agencies, within 120 days, of recommendations for an Open Government Directive, to be issued by the Director of OMB, that instructs executive departments and agencies to take specific actions implementing the principles set forth in this memorandum. The independent agencies should comply with the Open Government Directive.

This memorandum is not intended to, and does not, create any right or benefit, substantive or procedural, enforceable at law or in equity by a party against the United States, its departments, agencies, or entities, its officers, employees, or agents, or any other person.

This memorandum shall be published in the *Federal Register*.

BARACK OBAMA

73. http://my.barackobama.com (accessed on January 20, 2009).

74. Josh Catone, "How the Barak Obama Campaign Uses Wikis to Organize Volunteers," *ReadWriteWeb*, March 4, 2008, http://www.readwrite web.com/archives/barack_obama_campaign_central_desktop.php (accessed September 23, 2009).

75. Britt Blaser, David Weinberger, and Joe Trippi. "Digital Government Through Social Networks: A Natural Alliance?" *People and Place: Ideas That Connect Us* 1, no. 1 (February 1, 2009), http://www.peopleandplace .net.

76. Beth Simone Noveck, personal interview, January 15, 2009.

77. "Case Study: mybarackobama.com," http://www.bluestatedigital .com/casestudies/client/obama_for_america_2008 (accessed October 28, 2009).

78. Kevin Merritt, "How Obama Will Use Web Technology," Techcrunch, January 24, 2008, http://www.techcrunch.com/2009/ 01/24/how-obama-will-use-web-technology/ (accessed January 2, 2009).]

79. "Your Government: Open for Business in New Ways and New Places," http://www.whitehouse.gov/newmedia/ (accessed October 17, 2009).

80. "President Obama Launches Office of Public Engagement: A New Name, Mission for White House Liaison Office," May 11, 2009, www .whitehouse.gov/the_press_office/President-Obama-Launches-Office-of-Public-Engagement/ (retrieved October 17, 2009).

81. Kevin Merritt, see note 78.

82. "Copyright Policy," http://www.whitehouse.gov/copyright (accessed October 28, 2009).

83. Dan McSwain, "Wrapping Up the Citizen's Briefing Book," Change .gov, http://change.gov/newsroom/entry/wrapping_up_the_citizens_brief ing_book/ (accessed January 17, 2009).

84. Sam Stein, "Obama's Citizen's Briefing Book Changes the Flow of Information," *The Huffington Post*, January 15, 2009, http://www.huff ingtonpost.com/2009/01/15/obamas-citizens-briefing_n_158035.html (accessed September 30, 2009).

85. U.S. Environmental Protection Agency, "Protect the Environment," http://www.epa.gov (accessed April 20, 2009).

86. Open Government Initiative. "Transparency and Open Govern- ment," http://www.whitehouse.gov/open/ (accessed October 28, 2009).

87. "Open Government Directive, Phase 3: Drafting," www.mixedink. com/OpenGov/ (accessed June 22, 2009).

88. Beth Simone Noveck, *Wiki Government: How Technology Can Make Government Better, Democracy Stronger, and Citizens More Powerful* (Wash- ington, DC: Brookings Institution Press, 2009).

89. Ibid.

90. U.S. Environmental Protection Agency, "Monitoring and Assessing Water Quality," http://www.epa.gov/volunteer/ (accessed January 16, 2009).

91. U.S. Environmental Protection Agency, "Guidance for Volunteer Programs," http://www.epa.gov/owow/monitoring/ (accessed January 16, 2009).

92. Sarah Rose Engel, "The Effectiveness of Using Volunteers for Biolog- ical Monitoring of Streams," masters in entomology thesis, Virginia Polytechnic and State University, 2000.

93. David Lazer, "What Happens to the Obama Network after the Elec- tion," *Personal Democracy Forum: techPresident,* November 4, 2008, http:// www.personaldemocracy.com/blog/entry/2153/what_happens_to_the_ obama_network_after_the_election_1 (accessed September 23, 2009).

94. Dan Froomkin, "It's Time for a Wiki White House," *The Huffington Post*, November 25, 2008, http://www.huffingtonpost.com/dan-froom

kin/its-time-for-a-wiki-white_b_146284.html (accessed December 4, 2008).

95. Britt Blaser, David Weinberger, and Joe Trippi, "Digital Government through Social Networks: A Natural Alliance?" *People and Place: Ideas that Connect Us* 1, no. 1 (February 1, 2009) http://www.peopleandplace .net.

96. "Space Input to the Citizen's Briefing Book," January 13, 2009, blog posting, *NASA Watch*, http://www.nasawatch.com/archives/2009/01/ space_input_to.html (accessed January 17, 2009).

97. Daren Brabham, "Crowdslapping the Government: First Amendment Protections for the Crowd in Government Crowdsourcing Ventures." Paper presented at the annual meeting of the Association for Education in Journalism and Mass Communication, Marriott Downtown, Chicago, August 6, 2008, http://www.allacademic.com/meta/ p271801_index.html (accessed February 5, 2009).

98. Associated Press, "Perry Finds $3 Million for Border Cameras," *Khou. com*, November 19, 2007, http://www.khou.com/news/state/stories/ (accessed November 27, 2008).

99. "Wiki White House," a panel discussion at Google, Washington, DC, January 9, 2009, http://www.newamerica.net/events/2008/wiki_ white_house (accessed October 28, 2009).

100. Archon Fung, Mary Graham, and David Weil, *Full Disclosure: The Perils and Promise of Transparency* (New York: Cambridge University Press, 2007).

101. Paul Starr, "The Sunlight Solution," *The American Prospect*, May 20, 2007, http://prospect.org/cs/articles?article=the_sunlight_solution (accessed September 23, 2009).

102. "Impact on Issues: 2004–2006," *A Guide to Public Policy Positions* (League of Women Voters, 2005).

103. Jonathan Lemire, "Original Cable Guy," January 15, 2005, http://www.college.columbia.edu/cct_archive/jan05/features3.php (accessed on January 15, 2009).

104. See the entry Source Watch, "Sunlight Foundation," http://www.sourcewatch.org/index.php?title=Sunlight_Foundation (accessed January 11, 2009).

105. KAP's structure loosely resembles that of Mozilla. KAP (beta.knowledgeaspower.org) invites individuals to join small action groups that promote KAP's online services around the state. Volunteers can also take on managerial roles within the organization. KAP asks members to report any bug discovered in the Web site and to recommend additional online features and services.

106. Mozilla does not encourage long-term blind collaboration. The formal application process for commit privileges brings the volunteer programmer into the community dialog, so that a once-blind collaboration is publicized.

107. Michael Hauben and Ronda Hauben, *Netizens: On the History and Impact of Usenet and the Internet*, (Los Alamitos, CA: IEEE Computer Society Press, 1997).

108. "The Free Software Definition," see note 5.

109. Mozilla Project, see note 10.